Cut Funeral Costs

Save $1,000s on Every Funeral

VANCE FERRELL

Eagle Mountain
BOOKS

Cut Funeral Costs
  Save $1,000s on Every Funeral
by Vance Ferrell
Published by Eagle Mountain Books, Inc.
Box 440, Altamont, TN 37301 USA
Printed in the United States of America
Cover and Text Copyright © 2001
by Eagle Mountain Books, Inc.

ISBN 0-9713104-0-8

This book is valuable.

It can save you and your loved ones an immense amount of grief, pain, and money for years to come.

A very helpful reference book for older people and anyone who has older loved ones.

CONTENTS

— *PART ONE* —
ELIMINATE HOSPITAL TUBES
AVOID A LOT OF MISERY
IN YOUR FINAL MONTHS

Preparing for Death 10

Is Unending Treatment in Your Future?
10
Imprisoned in Tubes 11
Inside an Intensive Care Unit 13

Informed Consent 14
The Patient Should Be Told 14
His Permission Should Be Obtained 14
The Cruzan Decision 15

The Patient Self-Determination Act 15

Advance Directives: Guarding against
Unending Treatment 16
State Laws and Advance Directives 17

Durable Power of Attorney 17
State Laws Vary 18
Both Living Will and Power of Attorney
Needed 18

State Laws about Living Wills and Durable Power of Attorney   19

The Best Three-fold Combination   20
The Two Primary Points   20
Additional Paragraphs You May Want to Add   21

Where to Obtain State-Approved Living Will and Durable Power of Attorney Forms   23

What You Should Know about Living Trusts   24
Two Types of Living Trusts   25
Beware of Scams   26

When There Is no Advance Directive   26
One Tragedy among Thousands   27

Should You Consider a Hospice?   28
How Hospices Can Help You   29

How to Select a Good Nursing Home   30

— PART TWO —
CUT FUNERAL COSTS
SAVE $1,000s
ON EVERY FUNERAL

Introduction   32
Arrangement of Part Two   32
Even Congress Is Aware of the Problem   33

1 – Facts about Funeral Homes
The Coffin-Makers' Association   35
Learn Ahead of Time   35

When You Contact the Funeral Director 36

Wanting to Know Your Death Benefits   37
Information about Caskets   38
A Visit to the Funeral Home   39
Pricing Formulas   41
When Size Is a Problem   42
Sealer Caskets   42
Looking for the Best Casket   44
The Vault   46
Not Required by Law   47
Sealer Vaults   49
Embalming Not Usually Required   49
The Embalming Procedure   52
Flowers   54
Clergy   55
Monuments   56
Other Items and Services   56
Viewing vs. Visitation   58

Funeral Prices   58

Summarizing Prices   58
One Estimated Average   60
NFDA's Averages   60
IFIC Data   60
Sample: Houston Price Range   61
Sample: Mid-Range Washington, D.C. Price List   62
Sample: Houston Add-ons   63
Sample: Denver   63
Amount of Casket Markup   63

2 – Facts about Cemeteries and Mausoleums

Burial Plots   65
Other Cemetery Services   65
Opening and Closing the Grave   67

Procedure at the Grave 67
Perpetual Care 68
"Abandoned" Grave Lots 68
Read the Fine Print 68

Cemetery and Mausoleum Fees 69
Acreage Costs 69
Facts about Mausoleums 69
Average Cemetery Fees 70
Sample: Houston Basic Crypt 71

3 – What about Cremation?

All about Cremation 72
Boxes for Cremation 72
Cremation in a Casket 72
The Cremation Process 73
Your Right to Keep the Ashes 74
Your Right to Scatter the Ashes 75
Scattering vs. Burial 75
Making Extra on Cremations 75
Direct Cremation Firms 76
The Consolidators 77
The Neptune Society 78

Cremation Fees 80
Sample: Denver 80
Sample: One SCI Price 80
Sample: Neptune 80
Urn Prices: Wholesale and Retail 81
Rented Caskets 81

Should You Consider Cremation? 81
The Cost Factor 81
Other Factors to Consider 82
Cautions about Cremation 83
Lowest-cost Cremations 84
In Summary 85

The Biblical Factor 85
What Does the Bible Teach? 85
Cremation in the Bible 86
Jewish Burials in the Time of Christ 87

4 – If You Select the Funeral Industry to Provide the Care

Dangers in Pay-Ahead Contracts 87
Pay-ahead Plans 87
Medicaid Limits as a Factor 88
Beware of a Later Billing Clause 89
Cash Advance Items 89
Was the Money Really Put in Trust? 90
Beware of "Constructive Delivery" 91
Another Trick: Model Changes 91
The Company May Be Sold 92
Default Guarantees May Be Lacking 92
Draining the Trusts 92
Interest Charges 92
If You Cancel a Contract 92
Irrevocable Contracts 93
Eleven Questions to Ask 93
Should You Rely on an Insurance Policy? 94
Facts about a Totten Trust 95
The Pre-paid Funeral Fraud 96
More Scams 97

Eleven Ways to Cut Costs 97

Pre-Planning the Funeral Service 99

Funeral Checklist: Step-by-Step What to Do 100

5 – How to Skip the Funeral Industry Entirely

Seven Levels of Funeral Expense: Choose the One You Want   102

A Funeral Which By-passes the Funeral Industry   103
   Description of the Procedure   104
   Description of the Casket   107
   Private Burial   110
   If You Want to Explore This Possibility   110
   If Death Occurs in a Hospital   112
   If the Body Must Be Transported   113
   Special Problems   114
   Your Own Private Cemetery   114
   Non-Funeral Home Cremation   115
   Location of Crematories   115
   Pacemakers in a Cremation   115
   The Legal Next of Kin   116
   The Obituary Notice   116
   When a Private Funeral Is Not Difficult   116
   Three That Are Lowest in Cost   117

Preparing the Death Certificate Yourself   118

Organizing a Church Funeral Committee   126
   Nine Ways to Help Others   126

Facts about Organ Donations and Medical Gifts   129
   Body Donation   129
   Organ Transplants   130
   The Uniform Donor Card   130
   Other Facts about the Giving of Organs   132

Later Cremation   134
The Possibility of Rejection   134

Government Benefits for Deceased U.S. Veterans   135

6 – More Facts Worth Knowing

How the Memorial Societies Can Help You   137

Significant State Statutes   139
Which States Have Special Regulations?   140
Which States Permit Private Burial?   141

Learning about the Consolidators   143

The Federal Trade Commission's Funeral Rule   147
Limitations of the Funeral Rule   147
Helpful Requirements of the Rule   149
Specific Prohibitions   150
Inadequate Surveillance   151

The New York Consumer Affairs Report   151
Introduction to the Report   151
The Conglomerate Problem   152
Five Proposals   154

Organizations That Can Help You   155

Books and Other Written Materials   159

List of Memorial Societies   165
United States   165
Canada   178

Index   181

— PART ONE —

ELIMINATE HOSPITAL TUBES

AVOID A LOT OF MISERY IN YOUR FINAL MONTHS

PREPARING FOR DEATH

This book is about funerals. Why then is the first part about hospitals? Because, as you and your loved ones near the end of your lives, not only will there be funeral problems, but also hospital problems.

What is going to happen to you and your loved ones, when you enter the hospital for, what turns out to be, the last time? Will you face the misery of a miserable, painful tubed existence which continues on and on? a way of life that neither you nor anyone else seems able to stop?

IS UNENDING TREATMENT IN YOUR FUTURE?

Let us make it clear, at the beginning of this section, that we in no way favor suicide; but, when you and I become old, we should be permitted to die a natural death in peace, without being kept in misery in a hospital for months or years when there is no possible hope of recovery.

Medical technology has advanced to the point where the hospitals are able to keep people alive, on and on, in a miserable state of body tubes and ongoing suffering. Hospitals are today able to neutralize the effects of certain life-threatening diseases, without actually healing the patient. Patients are kept from dying, but also from living. Medical care should help people and heal them, not make them tied-down zombies.

Imprisoned in tubes. If the patient is very weak or permanently unconscious, medical technology dominates the situation, in spite of the wishes of the patient or his relatives

Tubes are temporarily put in till the patient strengthens; but then, when that does not happen, the tubes are left in and more are inserted.

Hospitals fear malpractice suits if they do not keep the tubes in the patient, even though he is laying there in misery with no possible chance of ever getting well.

The patient has ventilator tubes put in him because his lungs do not work properly. Because air passages no longer work properly, oral intubation occurs and he is hooked to a respirator. If the tube runs through the nose, sinusitis may result. If through the mouth, oral hygiene is difficult and he can no longer speak. The patient feels so terrible that he tries to tear out the tubes. To keep this from happening, he is partially sedated and his hands are tied down. If he wriggles around too much, his legs are tied down also. He lays there, imprisoned and feeling extremely uncomfortable, day after day. If he was locked up in a federal prison, he would have far more freedom.

Catheters are inserted to release urine from the bladder. Intravenous tubes are placed in his arms, or through a hole cut into his neck, to provide artificial nutrition and hydration. The most common is a nasogastric tube, a soft plastic tube that is run through the nose into the esophagus and then into the stomach. The patient gags as the tube is being inserted down the throat. It often produces a sore throat.

In the absence of other serious medical problems, and as long as he continues to breathe and have a functioning heart, this patient can stay alive almost indefinitely with artificial feeding.

And there is a continual danger of infection from the tubes. Once a person requires ICU-like interventions, the number of complications that can develop are many, leading to continued deterioration.

If the patient shows little interest in eating or remaining alive, a gastrostomy is the next step. A small hole is cut into the stomach and a feeding tube is inserted. This is called force feeding.

If the digestive tract is not working well, a catheter is inserted into a blood vessel, usually in the neck. The resulting tube provides the patient with "total parenteral nutrition" (TPN).

It can be very distressing for an older person with an acute, life-threatening illness to wake up in a hospital with hands tied and a tube inserted in his or her windpipe. And then, with the passing of weeks, more tubes are inserted.

No one will listen to his pleas, to remove the tubes; no one will listen to his family's pleas.

Inside an intensive care unit. Here is a peek inside an ICU:

"There is glass everywhere and little privacy. A deliberate design, it permits a small number of highly trained caregivers to provide constant and immediate care to a larger number of very sick patients.

"A second source of dismay can be the forest of tubes attached to the patient. Some of these, like the plastic IV (intravenous) tubes, bring medication or nourishment into the patient's bloodstream. Another, a nasogastric tube inserted through the nose, conveys liquid food directly into the patient's stomach. Yet another plastic tube, called a catheter, drains urine from the patient.

"Perhaps the most noticeable machine is the respirator, because it is so noisy. Designed to pump oxygen into the bloodstream, the respirator is extremely sensitive and needs to be adjusted frequently. If, for example, the patient's breathing pattern deviates from that of the respirator, an alarm will sound to alert the monitoring technician to make any necessary adjustments.

"Patients are under constant monitoring. Over each patient looms a camera connected to a video terminal at the nurses' station. A bedside monitor transfers an instant record of the patient's heartbeat to the nurses' terminal. Any significant change in rhythm will automatically trigger an alarm and alert the staff. In the event of cardiac arrest, a defibrillating machine and an external pacemaker are there for immediate use."—*T. Patrick Hill and David Shirley, A Good Death, p. 64.*

INFORMED CONSENT

In theory, the patient is supposed to be told in advance all that may happen, so he can give his written consent to the medical procedures which will take place. But, for decades, physicians have rarely informed their patients of a terminal diagnosis, thus depriving them of the possibility of having any say in how their treatment would be handled.

It was erroneously thought that the patient might prematurely die in despair if he was informed of a terminal diagnosis. Yet the patient needed to know what was ahead, so he could settle his estate and make other necessary plans.

The patient should be told. Patients in the hospital should know more about what is being done to them than animals in a barn are told when the veterinarian comes.

The patient should be told. He should be told the truth. He should be asked if he wants it done.

His permission should be obtained. But by the mid 1970s, in court case after court case, the legal principle of *informed consent* for terminally ill patients had been secured. It was the duty of the physician to inform the patient as to his condition, what needed to be done, and then receive the patient's permission to do it. That is *informed consent.* Informed consent had finally become a legal requirement. Keep that fact in mind. When you enter the hospital, you have a right to be correctly told your condition and to agree to the procedures which will be done.

The Cruzan decision. The U.S. Supreme Court's decision, in the 1990 case of *Missouri vs. Cruzan*, provides significant constitutional protection for patients who want to ensure that their wishes for—or against—life-sustaining treatment will be honored. The court ruled that a competent patient's right to refuse unwanted medical treatment is derived from our common-law traditions of bodily integrity and informed consent.

The Supreme Court essentially recognized the enforceability for *living wills*, *durable powers of attorney*, and other *advance directives* as protected by constitutional law.

THE PATIENT SELF-DETERMINATION ACT

On December 1, 1991, a new federal law went into effect. Known as the *Patient Self-Determination Act* (PSDA), it requires hospitals and skilled nursing facilities which receive Medicare or Medicaid funding to handle advance medical directives in very specific ways.

When the patient is first admitted, he has to be informed of his rights, under state law, to refuse medical and surgical treatment. He must also be informed of his right to prepare a living will and other advance directives. The fact that he has been given this information must immediately be placed on his chart.

However, depending on the internal policies of

the hospital or the attitudes of the nursing staff, advance directives may be fully honored—or partially or wholly ignored.

The best solution is for you, at some previous time, to have prepared your written, advanced directives and also to authorized someone as your proxy; that is, with durable power of attorney to speak in your behalf. In this way, you are far more likely to not have the tubes installed and be kept in place for long, terrible months while you are tied down with tubes in your body.

ADVANCE DIRECTIVES: GUARDING AGAINST UNENDING TREATMENT

Advance directives are written instructions placed in two main documents: a *living will* and a *health-care proxy* (that is, a *power of attorney authorization*). A living will contains future requests, regarding medical treatment, and a health-care proxy assigns someone to make future decisions, in case the person becomes unable to do so.

The concept of advance directives, regarding medical care, first began to emerge in the 1960s. Many people, fearful that they might later be subjected to body tubes in hospital beds for a seemingly unending period of time before they died, wrote letters to relatives in which they expressed their wishes.

But, since those letters were not detailed and precise and there was a question whether they were legally binding, physicians and hospitals tended to ignore them.

The truth is that no physician or other health-care provider has ever been successfully prosecuted for acting in accordance with a patient's written advance instructions, to forego life-sustaining treatment. Yet many physicians fear to obey such instructions. In the past, this was due to the fact that few states had made laws about informed consent.

State laws and advance directives. But, in recent years, due to the initially uncertain status of living wills and the inadequacy of many patients' advance handwritten statements, most states have enacted laws which not only approve of advanced medical directives, but have provided guidelines for their preparation and criteria for their use.

Many of these laws clearly express their objective to clarify (expand) the rights of the patient in making advance directives, in respect to the withholding or withdrawing of life-sustaining procedures.

But some state laws are so narrowly written that they greatly limit the medical conditions under which a living will can be obeyed by medical personnel. Some laws even limit the kinds of life-sustaining treatment a person can choose to forego. More on this soon.

Yet the *Cruzan* decision, made by the Supreme Court in 1990, clearly spelled out the patient's right to state in advance his wishes and the duty of the hospital to obey them.

DURABLE POWER OF ATTORNEY

A majority of states have expanded the rights of

incompetent patients, but recognizing the right of competent adults to authorize someone to make medical decisions. This is generally referred to as the *durable health-care power of attorney*. The rights of the person authorized, under durable power of attorney, to make medical decisions are usually the same as the rights of the person for whom the decisions are being made.

State laws vary. Because state laws vary in regard to this matter, we will list below those states which authorize power of attorney. Obviously, it is best if a state permits both advance directives and durable power of attorney, yet this is lacking in the laws of some states. A brief overview of those state laws is listed just below.

Both living will and power of attorney needed. By legally conferring on another person all the rights of the patient, through durable power of attorney, many of the problems and restrictions caused when a person becomes incompetent can be avoided. Thus it is best to not only fill out a living will (containing advance directives), but also the durable power of attorney form. Information on how to obtain copies of both will be given shortly.

Because it is sometimes difficult to get hospitals to do what should be done, it is far better if both the living will (with its advance directives) and the durable power of attorney have been earlier written.

Then, if the person becomes incompetent, the one having durable power of attorney for him can point to that person's previous wishes in the matter and say, "This is not only what I, his legal proxy, want to be done for him; but this is what he earlier specified, in his advance directives, should be done under these circumstances." That is more likely to encourage cooperation by the attending physicians and nurses.

It should be mentioned here that, in case you end up in a nursing home, there is a special need for you to have earlier made a living will and appointed someone to have durable power of attorney. Select that person carefully, for he must defend your wishes in the face of strong-minded nursing personnel, physicians, and the administration of the facility.

STATE LAWS ABOUT LIVING WILLS AND DURABLE POWER OF ATTORNEY

Specific aspects of laws, regarding living wills and medical-care legislation, varies greatly from state to state. To complicate the matter, court-made laws affecting the rights of the people have been made in many states. For specific information about your state, contact Choice in Dying, Inc. Just a few pages from here, we will give their address, phone numbers, and website.

In general, the *following states authorize both living wills / declarations and the appointment of a medical-care agent (the power of attorney factor):*

District of Columbia and 43 states: Arizona, Arkansas, California, Colorado, Connecticut, Delaware, Florida, Georgia, Hawaii, Idaho, Illinois, Indiana, Iowa, Kansas, Kentucky, Louisiana, Maine, Minnesota, Mississippi, Missouri, Montana, Nebraska, Nevada, New Hampshire, New Jersey, New Mexico, North Carolina, North Dakota, Ohio, Oregon, Pennsylvania, Rhode Island, South Carolina, South Dakota, Tennessee, Texas, Utah, Vermont, Virginia, Washington, West Virginia, Wisconsin, and Wyoming.

The following states have laws which only permit living wills / declarations, but do not mention the appointment of a medical-care agent: Alabama, Alaska, Maryland, and Oklahoma.

The following states authorize the appointment of a medical-care agent, but make no mention of living wills / declarations: Massachusetts, Michigan, and New York.

THE BEST
THREE-FOLD COMBINATION

The two primary points. Because the laws vary from state to state, it is important that both living wills and statements authorizing durable power of attorney closely adhere to existing state laws.

However, there may be additional aspects which you wish to specify—which go beyond the bounds of the law in your state. One example would be a rejection of artificial nutrition and hydration, in a state law that does not explicitly specify that you can refuse it. (That may seem to be a strange situation, in view of the 1991 federal law mentioned earlier—the *Patient Self-Determination Act*, which required hospitals and skilled nursing facilities which receive Medicare or Medicaid funding to handle advance medical directives in very specific ways. But the federal law works with state laws in governing the matter.)

If you do express your determination that additional things be done—or not done—beyond that expressly permitted by your state, you should specifically mention that your choices for treatment are based on an understanding of, and commitment to, the common-law principles of *bodily integrity*, *informed consent*, and *self-determination*.

Summarizing, the best plan is for you to (1) fill out a living will and (2) acquire durable power of attorney authorization which adheres to the laws of your state; (3) add other stipulations you have in mind, based on the common-law principles of bodily integrity, informed consent, and self-determination. That combination of a living will, an appointed legal proxy, and a written appeal to the broadest possible interpretation of common and constitutional law—will go a long way toward ensuring that your wishes will be honored later in life, when you so much need them done.

Additional paragraphs you may want to add. It is important that you decide whether you should include a DNR (do not resuscitate) paragraph in your living will. It would say something like this: "I do not want my life prolonged artificially, if I have an incurable and irreversible condition. I do not want to be resuscitated under any circumstances. I do not want my heart restarted with CPR or failed breathing restored with a mechanical breathing machine." Once the physician enters a DNR order on the chart, there is a good chance it will be respected, even in a crisis. (The problem is getting it onto the chart.) Do-not-resuscitate orders vary from state to state, and they must always be signed by a physician. But, unless you have previously made the DNR statement, the physician will not later agree to it. Each hospital has its own DNR form. A separate form is available for non-hospital situations (if you are dying at home). A 1995 study, published in the *Journal of the American Medical Association*, found that nearly half the wishes of all dying patients who asked their doctors to issue DNR orders were ignored (*JAMA 277, November 22, 1995*).

Here are five specific sentences, one or more of which you might wish to add to your living will:

"I do not wish to be attached to a mechanical breathing machine."

"I do not wish to have my heart resuscitated with medications and mechanical methods."

"I do not wish to be fed with a feeding tube."

"I do not wish to be given fluid hydration with intravenous lines."

"I do not wish to be given antibiotics."

You should conclude the paragraphs you have selected with the statement: "My choices for treatment are based on an understanding of, and commitment to, the common-law principles of bodily integrity, informed consent, and self-determination."

Another sentence you might wish to add, in the hope that later conditions and an available helper would later make it possible, is this: "I want to die at home." Andrea Ankar has a complete book on this subject: *Dying at Home: A Family Guide for*

Caregiving.

Yet another sentence could be this one: "I want to die at home or in a hospice." More on hospices shortly.

WHERE TO OBTAIN STATE-APPROVED LIVING WILL AND DURABLE POWER OF ATTORNEY FORMS

Consideration was given to including a sample living will and durable power of attorney in this book, so you could see what they look like. But some readers might misunderstand and use them. It is imperative that you only use the forms which agree with laws in your own state.

In order to obtain those needed state-specific forms, contact a local hospital, your state capital, or Choice in Dying, Inc.

Choice in Dying is now the largest and strongest right-to-die organization in the world, with 150,000 members in the United States alone. Dedicated to ensuring individual freedom and compassionate care at the end of life. It works to educate physicians, nurses, attorneys, clergy, and the public. It assisted in drafting the Patient Self-Determination Act, which was enacted by Congress in 1991.

You would do well to contact Choice in Dying for a current copy of your state's living will and durable power of attorney. Here is how to obtain these forms:

Choice in Dying: 475 Riverside Drive, Room 1852, New York, NY 10115. Phones: 800-989-9455

/ 212-870-2003. They mail out thousands of copies each year. The cost is $5.00 ppd. for a copy of your state's living will and durable power of attorney.

An alternative is to go to their website:
partnershipforcaring.org
and download, free of charge, copies of your state's living will and durable power of attorney.

You may wish to inquire about their Living Will Registry. By joining it, they will ensure that your form is filled out correctly, assign you a registry number, maintain a copy of your living will, and issue you a plastic card which you can carry with you at all times so medical personnel can know where to obtain a copy of your living will and power of attorney authorization. Any current changes you may wish to make can be sent to them. The cost is about $40.

WHAT YOU SHOULD KNOW ABOUT LIVING TRUSTS

Living trusts are quite different than living wills. Living trusts are legal statements which decide what is to happen to your estate (your property) after your death.

Living trusts are a way to avoid probate, the procedure which determines the distribution of a deceased person's property, regardless of whether there is a will. A living trust avoids probate because at the time of death the trust, not the deceased, owns the assets. Only property in the deceased's name must go through probate.

In a living trust, assets including savings accounts, real estate, and securities are put into the trust while the owner is still alive. Legal title to the assets is transferred to a trustee, and the owner can name himself or herself as the trustee. The trust contains instructions for handling assets during the owner's lifetime and distributing them after death.

Because the laws, the costs, and the amount of time affecting both probate and trusts vary from state to state, consumers should contact a reputable local attorney or estate planner, to discuss their personal situation. Depending on individual circumstances, a living trust may be a good option; however, it is not for everyone.

Two types of living trusts. There are two types of trusts, revocable and irrevocable. A revocable trust can be changed or revoked at any time during the owner's lifetime. An irrevocable trust cannot be recalled or abolished after its creation. There are advantages and disadvantages to both.

The advantage of an irrevocable trust is that it cannot be changed by your heirs after your death. But you may not, prior to death, be able to change it yourself! Conditions in life can change!

The revocable trust is safer for you while you are alive; the irrevocable trust is safer for keeping your property from those whom you do not want it to go to, after you die.

A living trust can include durable power, and you should be aware of the dangers. The present writer is acquainted with two instances in which families set up a living trust to bequeath their property to an organization. In both instances, the trust officer did not do right by them later in life. So problems can develop.

Beware of scams. Probate may be a costly, time-consuming process, although that is not true in every case. However, some salespeople paint living trusts as a magical cure for all estate planning, making probate look like an expensive and very agonizing process. Often the do-it-yourself kits are nothing more than form-letter type documents which do not automatically transfer consumers' assets into the trust and may have no standing in court. Better Business Bureaus report that consumers are being pressured to sign contracts on the spot and write checks for hundreds, sometimes thousands, of dollars to establish a living trust.

Scam artists, masquerading as experts, will offer to plan your living trust. They will try to scare you with stories of long, expensive probate, tax increases on the horizon, family fights, and fees equal to a huge percentage of the total estate.

If you believe a living trust is the best solution, do not be taken in by fraudulent offers and extravagant promises from fly-by-night operators. Instead, consult with a trusted adviser or contact your local Better Business Bureau for a reliability report.

WHEN THERE IS NO
ADVANCE DIRECTIVE

You should be aware of the fact that, even though the patient made out a living will, it may be ignored by the medical staff at the hospital—if there is not an aggressive friend or family member to intervene. But they need to have in hand the written request (living will) of the patient. Otherwise it would be difficult for relatives to convince the hospital to turn off a respirator or stop force-feeding, even though the outlook is admittedly hopeless. But, if a friend or family member also has durable power of attorney, that greatly helps to clinch the demand that the wishes of the patient be fulfilled.

One tragedy among thousands. Here is an incident, written by a medical doctor, which illustrates the problem:

"Without written documentation [an advance directive statement by the person himself], you are helpless against doctors or family members who don't respect your wishes. I remember too vividly the last days of my grandmother Bobby . . She was vibrant and full of life. She told me that, when her time came, she wanted to go out with no fuss, with no machines keeping her body alive artificially. To her, this was so logical that she assumed everyone else would agree: she trusted that common sense would prevail when she reached her dying . .

"[Decades later at the nursing home] a medical resident recognized her breathing difficulty and immediately placed a tube in her mouth, through her throat, and into her lungs. The tube attached her to an artificial breathing machine called a ventilator. She was then tethered to the machine, with her arms and legs tied to restrain her [because she felt so terrible with the tubes in her]. This is a common procedure, as patients will attempt to remove breathing tubes, intravenous tubes, and other apparatus in their confusion and pain.

"My brother called me, upset with the decision to place this ninety-four-year-old woman on a ventilator. I was shocked . . I immediately called my mother and uncle. They didn't feel competent to challenge the medical authorities. 'We're letting the doctors do what they think is best,' they told me.

"I then called Bobby's supervising medical doctor, who explained that when she came to the emergency room there were no advance directives with her, so they were legally obligated to do everything to keep her alive. To get her off the ventilator, Bobby's children would have to file a complicated appeal, which they wouldn't do . .

"Bobby had a strong heart, which kept her alive, alone in a strange hospital room, attached to a bunch of machines, for over six and a half months. Finally, mercifully, she died."—*Daniel R. Tobin, M.D., Peaceful Dying, pp. 87-89.*

SHOULD YOU CONSIDER A HOSPICE?

We can be very thankful for the efforts of Cecily Sauders, in Britain; Elizabeth Kubler-Ross, in the United States; and all the others who have worked with them, to pave the way for hospice care to be started and integrated into our medical system.

The hospice plan provides careful attention to pain control, as well as loving comfort in one's final months. The work of hospices is based on the thinking that it may be desirable to stop attempts to cure disease when death is approaching and inevitable. The hospices pioneered the concept of death with dignity and humane pain management. They let a person have the right to die in peace.

It has only increased public demand for procedures that allow death with dignity; this forced the medical establishment to become less resistant to hospices.

For many persons, faced with the last stages of a terminal illness, hospice care offers the best setting in which to have their wishes for end-of-life treatment honored.

Since 1980, hospices have spread all across America. Gradually, more and more people are choosing hospices instead of hospital wards or intensive care units, as the place to spend their final days.

Although England specializes in hospices with in-house care, in America there are more home-care hospice programs to help those who wish to die at home than there are hospices with in-patient care.

How hospices can help you. It is an interesting fact that the information you have written down on your advance directives—exactly matches the care you will receive if your final days are in a hospice. They use no "artificial or heroic means" to keep you alive. They reduce pain, make you as comfortable as possible, and provide relief from the distressing symptoms of terminal illness. But they do not sustain life by artificial means.

Only those who have accepted the inevitability of death go to a hospice. Hospices are limited, by Federal hospice Medicare benefits, to only taking patients with (1) no expected cure and (2) a prognosis of less than six months to live.

Each hospice has its own rules, and some are quite rigid. Some will provide tubes for hydration or nutrition if (if) the patient requests; others definitely will not. But there are no surprises later; you will know exactly what the hospice rules are before you enter it.

Since much hospice care is home care, hospice consent forms routinely stipulate that another person outside the hospice team must identify himself or herself as a primary caretaker for the patient, to manage ongoing care when the hospice team is not present—and to care for all the financial and household duties of the patient. That person must have durable power of attorney for the patient. That person must also be acquainted with state health-care-proxy (power of attorney) laws.

For more information, you may wish to contact one or more of the following:

American Hospice Foundation: 1130 Connecticut Avenue NW, Suite 700, Washington, D.C. 20036-4101. Phone: 202-223-0204

Hospice Association of America: 519 C Street NE, Stanton Park, Washington, D.C. 20002-5809. Phone: 202-546-4750

National Hospice Organization: 1901 North Moore Street, Suite 901, Arlington, VA 22209. Phone: 703-243-5900

Hospice Education Institute, Five Essex Square: P.O. Box 713, Essex, CT 06426 Phone: 800-331-1620

HOW TO SELECT A GOOD NURSING HOME

Do not take things for granted. Just because a nursing home is nearby or looks nice, does not mean a loved one will be provided proper care. Check ahead of time! Here are some pointers:

• *Do a background check:* Phone your local or state health-care agency or long-term-care ombudsman. (You can find yours by calling the Eldercare Locator at 800-677-1116.) Ask if there have been any complaints against the facility you are interested in. Be sure it is licensed or certified.

• *Visit the place:* Arrive unannounced, and at least once at night. Look around without a staff person by your side. Talk to residents and their families. Ask how long it takes for staff to respond to a call bell. Observe how caregivers behave. Eat a meal. Look for smiles. Are the residents happy? Are regularly scheduled activities provided?

• *Inquire about the quality of the staff:* Ask questions. How much training and prior experience will the primary caregiver for my family member have? How many caregivers actually show up for work on each shift, especially at night? How much turnover is there? Are criminal background checks conducted on prospective employees? How much time does a registered nurse spend on site? If there is an emergency, what is the staff (especially the nighttime shift) trained to do?

• *Plan for the future:* Does the facility have experience in providing adequate care for severe ailments, including dementia and Alzheimer's?

• *Beware of escalating fees:* The basic fee at many facilities only covers room and board. The rest may cost extra (baths, dispensing of medications, and lifts out of bed). As many patients become more ill, many facilities increase the charges.

• *Get it in writing:* The residency agreement you sign should be clear and comprehensive. It should spell out exactly what care is, and is not, included. Be sure the agreement details precisely under what conditions residents are asked to leave.

— PART TWO —
CUT FUNERAL COSTS
SAVE $1,000s
ON EVERY FUNERAL

INTRODUCTION

The Bible explains, in very clear words, what is to happen at death: "In the sweat of thy face shall thou eat bread, till thou return unto the ground; for out of it wast thou taken; for dust thou art, and unto dust shalt thou return."—*Genesis 3:19.*

If we keep that principle clearly in mind, we can make better choices when confronted by all the modern ways provided to put our beloved dead back into the ground,—and we can avoid the many expensive methods devised to keep them from returning, as God intended, to the ground.

Burying the dead is the third largest expense in the lives of most people. But, unlike the purchase of homes and automobiles, death comes unexpectedly and leaves us very vulnerable to men who are anxious to profit on our grief.

Arrangement of Part Two. This part of the

book is designed to provide you with information you need to know ahead of time. Armed with this information, before the death of a loved one suddenly arrives, you can begin making preparations. You will be able to decide for yourself what you want to do.

America is full of fine people and there are many good undertakers and cemeteries. But, in case you might encounter one that is different, this book can provide you with valuable information which may save you money and needless grief.

First we will consider funeral homes. Then we will discuss cemeteries and mausoleums, and after that, cremation. Then we will tell you how to conduct your own burial of a loved one—by-passing the funeral industry entirely. Still more information follows that. The book concludes with sources you can contact for further information and a list of nonprofit organizations which may be able to direct you toward lower-cost funeral options.

Even Congress is aware of the problem. By 2001, the United States had 22,000 funeral homes. The average undertaker's bill, which was $750 in 1961, for casket and "services,"—is now over $7,000. But that does not include a variety of other costs—including a burial vault, clothing, flowers, and cemetery charges. The total average cost for an adult funeral today is over $7,800.

You are going to learn some of the ways that some funeral directors and cemetery owners lock people into paying a lot of money, which they cannot afford to spend.

To introduce the subject, here is an interesting

quotation from a brokerage house, analyzing the prospects of the funeral industry as a place stock investors should consider:

"The addition of well-chosen death care stocks to an investment portfolio can increase the value of that portfolio nicely. Consumers rarely comparison shop due to the infrequency of purchase, which averages once in every 14 years. In many instances, a deceased's survivors will trade up for more expensive options than what may have already been prearranged."—*Chicago Corporation investment brochure.*

Does that tell you a few things? It should.

On April 11, 2000, Congress held hearings on funeral homes in America. What is happening is fast becoming a scandal, and it is becoming more widely known. One lady in Florida was talked into spending $132,000 on a funeral.

There are both funeral homes and cemeteries. Each one frequently has separate charges. "Cemeteries" are graveyards, and "mausoleums" are buildings with "crypts" (caskets) in them. In this book, "cemeteries" will sometimes include mausoleums. The words, "mortuaries" and "mortuary establishments," generally refer to cemeteries and mausoleums; but, in some literature, it can include funeral homes. The "funeral industry" includes the entire professional death industry.

We will first consider funeral homes and, then, turn our attention to cemeteries and mausoleums. After that, we will learn about the advantages and disadvantages of cremation.

1 – FACTS ABOUT FUNERAL HOMES

The coffin-makers' association. Early in our nation's history, coffins were often manufactured as a sideline by furniture makers. Many of these folk also began working as undertakers on the side. (The word *"undertaker"* simply means an individual who undertakes to prepare a body for burial.) The burial business continued in this haphazard way into the late 19th century.

But then companies came into existence which specialized in making coffins. Iserson, in his book *Death to Dust*, explains that the coffin makers quickly organized themselves into the National Burial Case Association—and then, in 1881, raised the price of coffins by 40%.

Shocked at the news, the undertakers organized their own trade association, so they could collectively bargain with the casket companies. Thus, market control by the funeral homes got off to an early start.

Learn ahead of time. According to a 1995 study done by the Wirthlin Group, at the request of the funeral industry, almost 90% of the public do not shop around for lower prices, etc. They just go to one funeral home. Many of them just follow that funeral director's suggestions, and that is it. The Wirthlin research found that 45% select a funeral home that previously served someone else in the family, 33% call the nearest mortuary (sometimes the only one in town), and 11% pick a funeral home that agrees with their ethnic or religious affiliation.

When it comes to funerals, the consumer is at a strong disadvantage, for it is only very infrequently that he makes decisions about a funeral. In a system which invites abuse, you just do not have opportunity to practice managing funerals. Therefore, it is wise to learn certain facts ahead of time.

An interesting book is Thomas Lynch's, *The Undertaking: Life Studies from the Dismal Trade*, published in 1997. Lynch, an undertaker in Milford, Michigan, dares to give you a peek inside a funeral home.

"In a good year, the gross is close to a million, five percent of which we hope to call profit. I am the only undertaker in this town. I have a corner on the market."

Five percent of a million is $50,000. Funeral directors, even in the smallest towns in America, are not going hungry.

WHEN YOU CONTACT THE FUNERAL DIRECTOR

The funeral home does not like to quote prices over the phone. They would rather that you come in, so they can show you all the various things they want to sell you. (However, if you are persistent over the phone, some will send you price lists.)

They can send a salesman to visit you in your home, to show you colored pictures and get you to sign a contract. But they prefer for you to come to the funeral home. Either way, you will gently be directed toward a complete and expensive funeral.

But they prefer to see you in person. When you arrive at a funeral home, the car you drive and how well you dress will quickly be assessed. If you are busy, the funeral director will eagerly offer to come to your home, so he can see what it looks like.

Wanting to know your death benefits. One of the first things the funeral director, or his salesman, will want to know is the possible death benefits. The undertaker knows the death-benefit payments provided by every trade union in the community. He knows the Social Security and workmen's compensation scale of death benefits. This helps him extract as much as possible out of each client. As part of his paid "services," he will have his secretary fill out the forms applying for this benefit for you. But you could save some money and easily do it yourself.

The Social Security payment is about $255. If the deceased was a veteran, a total of $555, plus, if selected, a free burial in a national cemetery (the person must die in a veteran's hospital in order to get the extra $300). If the death was occupationally connected, some state workers' compensation laws will provide an additional funeral allowance of up to $5,000. There are also trade union benefits and various insurance benefits.

This extra cash suddenly in the hand of the grieving survivor makes him more welcome to the funeral director's suggestions. (He also knows that, under the law of virtually every state, the funeral bill is entitled to preference in payment as the first charge against the estate.)

Information about caskets. What is the difference between a casket and a coffin? Only the price. *Webster's New Twentieth Century Dictionary, Unabridged,* gives the definition of a casket: "A coffin, especially a costly one."

The lowest-cost caskets are made of wooden particle board, covered with cloth. Next up are the plain pine caskets, commonly used for the burial of orthodox Jews and constructed without any metal whatsoever. Instead of screws, they are fastened with wood dowels and glue. About 10% of all caskets sold are wooden.

More expensive still are those of hardwood (oak, walnut, cherry, mahogany, etc.). About 15% of the public purchase grained-hardwood caskets. These are made in a style which looks like fine furniture.

But the funeral director pushes the metal ones, since he sells them for much more. Oddly enough, the metal ones cost less to manufacture.

The lowest-cost metal ones are made of 20-gauge steel and are so thin they can easily be dented. More expensive ones contain thicker steel (18- or 16-gauge).

Steel caskets are welded and often spray painted. Frequently, the bottom is cheaper gauge steel and only spot welded. The whole thing is designed to last only a few days, before it starts falling apart.

The finest metal caskets are made of bronze or copper and comprise only 3% of all caskets sold. They are not welded, but are cast from molds. With these, as with all caskets, the "accessories" (the lining, mattress, pictures, sculpted additions) increase the price still higher.

Only 1% of the caskets sold are made of plastic, aluminum, or fiberglass. They are quite inexpensive and many funeral directors refuse to stock them. Oddly enough, the lowly plastic caskets survive the longest in the ground. They do not rust or rot.

The price of a casket is based on many things: material, finish, hardware, lining, mattress, style. ("Style" means whether it is "full couch," allowing viewing of the entire body, or "half counch," permitting viewing from the waist up.)

Low-cost caskets contain mattresses and pillows filled with sawdust or wood shavings. Pay enough and you can have an inner-spring adjustable mattress! No kidding!

Inexpensive materials, such as rayon, are used to line lower-cost caskets. The higher-priced ones are luxuriously upholstered in a much more expensive material, such as satin or velvet, that is often sewn in intricate design patterns.

The hardware (the handles and hinges) can also vary in price, as can the addition of pictures displayed on the underside of the lid (the Last Supper, praying hands, flowers, etc.). Various sculpted designs can be attached to the top of the casket.

A visit to the funeral home. Arriving at the funeral home, you will first be shown the caskets. These will generally be in a room by themselves, with medium to high prices. In some localities, you will be taken from the top, on down. A minister in Berkeley, California, Laurence Cross, describes how the funeral director sells the casket to the grieving relative:

"First, you come to a magnificent casket—it's like a pink show window. You'd think it had the Queen's jewels on display. The inside is made of beautiful satin and it's set out on a thick white carpet. You walk along and come to the next one. There's another beauty, maybe in a different pastel shade. You see a few more, and then you come to the absolute end. There aren't any more. Those you have seen are priced very high."

Only very expensive caskets are shown, nothing else. Pastor Cross describes what the sorrowful loved one replies:

" 'I hadn't planned to spend that much, but since these are my only options, I guess I'll have to get one.' Only the bold tell the undertaker that his goods are outside their price range and that they'll have to go somewhere else.

"For those few bold bereaved, however, the funeral director opens a door *you never knew existed*. You go into another room where there are maybe half a dozen caskets—in less attractive colors than the other beauties—and at somewhat lower prices. That's where the psychology comes in. The average person who has managed to avoid the more expensive caskets now feels that at least he has saved several hundred dollars. But if you're mean as the devil, you may still insist that the caskets you've seen are more than you were prepared to pay.

"So you go through the same procedure. The funeral director opens *yet another door* you never knew existed, and here are some for even less. If you are still so mean that you won't spend that much, you are led into the last room. Here the funeral director . . shows you an ugly casket, maybe purple in color. The cheap ones are purposely made up in hideous colors, and they have no handles, no lining.

"If you still won't buy that, you are taken from there through a concrete alleyway as dark as Egypt. You come to a garage where all the funeral cars are parked. Then he pulls out a box. It's just six pieces of redwood nailed together . . He'll charge anything he can get out of you for it."—*Laurence Cross, Berkeley Community Church, Berkeley, California [emphasis his], quoted in Christianity Today, April 26, 1999.*

Pricing formulas. The significance to the consumer of wholesale casket costs lies in the use of, what the trade calls, "pricing formulas." The price of the entire funeral is arrived at by marking up the wholesale casket cost anywhere from 400% to as much as 900% or higher. The markup is usually steepest in the lower price ranges.

The entire funeral industry jealously guards their wholesale casket, and other, prices. So do not expect them to tell you.

Morticians (another name for the funeral home director) may tell you that you must, by law, purchase the casket from them. But that is not true. Or they may tell you that they must impose a "casket handling fee" if you buy the casket somewhere else.

In those instances in which the funeral home director must compete with a nearby casket firm, he lowers his casket prices while at the same time raising his service fees.

It is sometimes possible to rent a casket. This will save you a lot of money. Some funeral directors place a plastic casket inside the rented casket, and then, at the cemetery, lift out the plastic casket and bury that. Others use a cardboard casket. (Cardboard caskets are most commonly used for shipping remains across the country.)

When size is a problem. Caskets come in a variety of shapes and materials. They also come in several sizes, but funeral directors generally do not stock larger sizes. Roberts, a former owner of funeral homes and cemeteries, explains:

> "Funeral directors are creative folks, though, and they can usually find ways to 'make do' with what's in stock. What do they do? For a very tall individual, the funeral director may be able to bend the legs or may remove the shoes to make the body fit into the box. For an obese individual with a protruding belly, the funeral director may turn the body slightly to one side and may position the hands further down so the lid can be closed."—*Darrell J. Roberts, Profits of Death, p. 34.*

In her 1963 book, *The American Way of Death*, Jessica Mitford related how a widow told her about a funeral director who did have a longer box on hand for her tall husband. But he said it would cost considerably more. When she replied that she could not afford it, the funeral director said that, if she did not pay for a longer box, he would have to cut the legs off. Shocked, she paid the extra money. But it was years before she told anyone about the devastating experience.

Sealer caskets. The funeral director will try to sell you a metal casket rather than a wooden one. The best one, and very ornate, is a "sealer casket" (also called a "gasketed" or "protective" casket). The wholesale price of a sealer casket is $350 while a cloth-covered softwood costs him about $160. But your price, of course, will be much higher. What is it that the casket needs to be sealed against? And how good is the warranty, since no one is going to check later to see if it leaks?

Keep in mind that, just as embalming forestalls only momentarily the natural process of decomposition, there is no casket nor grave vault that will keep out the elements for all time.

These so-called "protective caskets" have been heavily merchandised over the years. They now outsell all other burial containers combined. Ask a funeral director why someone already dead will need protection and he will reply, "To prevent alien and foreign objects from reaching your loved one."

Protective caskets, which command substantially higher prices than those that are "unprotected," achieve protection by using an impermeable—but very inexpensive—rubber gasket as a sealing device.

After the lid of the casket is closed, the funeral director then turns internal screw mechanisms in the casket, which tighten the lid into a neoprene gasket.

The high price you will be charged for that gasket may bother you. The rubber gasket costs the industry about $8, but it may add $800 to the price paid by the consumer. There is something else which should concern you: Because the casket is sealed, a buildup of methane gas occurs, a by-product of the metabolism of anaerobic bacteria which, thriving in an airless environment, produce immense pressure. This eventually warps the casket and frequently cracks it open (*i.e.*, causes it to explode).

Instead of the natural dehydration that would otherwise occur, the body putrefies in the anaerobic environment. The funeral industry knows all about this, but they do not want you to know.

(Sealer caskets that are placed in mausoleums or above-ground crypts are routinely unsealed after the family leaves, to make sure it does not later explode.) Roberts, a former funeral director, explains what happens when they forget to unscrew the seal:

"Several weeks after a body was placed in a sealed casket and put into the mausoleum, the body exploded with such force that it destroyed the casket and blew the marble front off the crypt. A mortician was called in to clean up the pieces of the body and place them in a new casket, after which the crypt was repaired. Obviously, the family was never notified."—*Darryl J. Roberts, Profits of Death, p. 44.*

When Queen Elizabeth I of England died, developments beyond her control caused her sealed, lead-lined coffin to lie in Whitehall for 34 days before burial. During this time, reported one of the ladies-in-waiting who sat as a watcher, the body "burst with such a crack that it split the wood, lead, and cerecloth; whereupon the next day she was fain [had to be] to be new trimmed up."

Looking for the best casket. Contrary to all the advertising claims, sales pitches, and implied warranties, there is nothing that can prevent the ultimate disintegration of the casket nor stop the flow of water into a vault. Yet it is just such implied claims that persuade the consumer to frequently over-spend, in the belief he is buying some kind of protection for the departed, which will help the deceased "be as comfortable as possible."

What is the best casket? A plain, wooden casket will fulfill the Bible injunction. "In the sweat of thy face shalt thou eat bread, till thou return unto the ground; for out of it wast thou taken; for dust thou art, and unto dust shalt thou return."—*Genesis 3:19*. A wooden casket will help fulfill this plan the most efficiently, and at the least expense. Does Heaven want us to spend thousands in caring for the dead or in providing for the living?

Since most people are buried in metal (as opposed to wood) caskets, how strong are they? The costliest caskets are those built of the thickest metal. The cheaper lines of metal caskets, constructed of thin sheet metal over a wooden frame, achieve the same look of massive elegance and can hardly be distinguished (except by pallbearers) from the heavyweights that sell for thousands of dollars more. A writer in *Mortuary Management* described the average run of lightweight metal caskets as "nothing more or less than stovepipe material."

The funeral industry is well-aware of the tendency for the survivors to select one level above the cheapest caskets. The Loewen Group, a conglomerate discussed later in this report, may set a higher price on the lowest-priced caskets. In this way, the next price level up, will provide them with more profit per funeral.

The Federal Trade Commission's "Funeral Rule" makes it illegal for morticians to tout the preservative qualities of a casket. But some do it anyway, by talking of their "protective" caskets.

If you want to find a low-cost casket of your choice, available for overnight delivery from a casket retailer or woodworker, for information, contact: funerals.org/famsa/caskets.htm.

The vault. We have considered the casket. Next comes the vault. This is a rectangular 4-inch thick concrete box and lid. The best have a 1/8-inch precast asphalt inner liner plus extra-thick, reinforced concrete. Sometimes the vault is made of steel. The casket is placed inside the vault, and both are buried in the cemetery.

Great lyric prose has been written about this box that will be buried in the ground:

"The quality and elegance usually reserved for higher priced vaults. Inspired by the strength and elegance that is classic Greek architecture, the Eagle Corinthian combines over sixty-five years of master craftsmanship with state-of-the-art technology. And like the great ancient columns, the Eagle Corinthian has been designed to offer the protection and durability that will stand the test of time . . Consider the Corinthian, uniquely affordable, yet offering the peace of mind that is truly priceless."—*Advertisement sent to funeral directors to display, Eagle Corinthian Burial Vault, Eagle Burial Vaults, Detroit, Michigan.*

Many cemeteries now require that the casket be placed in a vault. Frequently, especially in urban areas, the funeral home and the cemetery compete to be first to sell you that vault (and frequently the casket as well).

Are there any advantages to the vault? The only

one is that, many, many decades from now, the wooden caskets will rot and the metal ones will rust and collapse. When the casket is inside a vault, that sinking of the ground above the burial plot does not occur. But the vault will cost you a lot of money which could be spent to provide for the needs of the living.

Not required by law. You may be told that the vault is required by law. Yet, if you contact the state office, you will probably learn that no such law exists. Some cemeteries, receiving cutbacks from the funeral homes, require that all caskets buried on their grounds be in vaults.

Although the vault is not required by state law, most cemeteries now refuse to accept burials which are not caskets to be placed in vaults.

As mentioned earlier, funeral homes also send salesmen to interview prospects in their homes, show them pictures, and get them to sign contracts. One individual, who knew the kind of information in this book, entered into the following conversation:

"In response to my inquiry, a cemetery salesman (identified on his card as a 'Memorial Counselor') called at my house to sell me what he was pleased to call a 'pre-need memorial estate'; in other words, a grave for future occupancy. After he quoted the prices of the various graves, the salesman explained that a minimum of $520 must be added for a vault, which, he said, is 'required by law.'

" 'Why is it required by law?'

" 'To prevent the ground from caving in.'

" 'But suppose I should be buried in one of those Eternal caskets made of solid bronze?'

" 'Those things are not as solid as they look. You'd be surprised how soon they fall apart.'

" 'Are you sure it is required by law?'

" 'I've been in this business fifteen years; I should know.'

" 'Then would you be willing to sign this?' (I had been writing on a sheet of paper, 'California state law requires a vault for ground burial.')

"The Memorial Counselor gathered up his color photographs of memorial estates and walked out of the house."—*Quoted in Lauren F. Winner, "Death, Inc.," Christianity Today, April 26, 1999.*

Some states restrict who may sell a vault. For example, in Tennessee, nobody but a funeral director may sell a vault. New Jersey prohibits cemeteries from selling vaults or memorial markers. But, in most states, cemeteries that do sell such items may not forbid you from purchasing them elsewhere.

When considering such a sizeable investment, keep this in mind: The customer rarely ever sees the actual vault, for it is normally selected from a catalog and is already in the ground when the graveside ceremony takes place. So you are not certain what is there. When the graves are closed, vaults are frequently damaged and even broken as the ground is compacted flat above them by heavy equipment after the funeral. Vaults are nothing more than concrete or metal boxes. No vault is impervious to eventual disintegration, and nothing placed underground ever remains waterproof.

Sealer Vaults. To add to the nonsense, some funeral directors will suggest that "sealer vaults" be provided for "additional protection." Instead of letting the dead return to the earth as the Lord intended, men are anxious to place them in sealer caskets—inside sealer vaults! But those are the vaults which pop out of the ground and float away during floods. Gravediggers, who have to move cemeteries, would much prefer to work in an older part of the cemetery where digging reveals rich loam; the casket and contents have been absorbed into the soil, unhindered by modern caskets and vaults. But when they have to open a metal casket, sealer casket, vault, or sealer vault, they have a terrible mess to work with. This is not as God intended. His plans are always the best.

The funeral home is not likely to mention that, if the vault must later be moved, drainage holes will have to be knocked in the bottom to let out all the water that has seeped in. When floods occur, those vaults which did not fill with water—float to the surface. The solution, of course, is to knock holes in the bottom and let in sink.

Embalming not usually required. The funeral home director will be anxious that you have your loved one embalmed, even though this will not be necessary since the burial will be very soon.

Embalming is not normally required by law, in America, for most deaths. In a few states, embalming may be necessitated by law when death occurs from a communicable disease. Normally, embalming is required only if the body is to be shipped across state or international boundaries.

Some states require that bodies be embalmed if burial is not going to occur within a certain number of days. If there is to be a delay prior to burial, some states do not require embalming if the body is refrigerated and taken from the cooler for no more than two or three hours in order to have a viewing, or if there is a closed-casket service.

But, whether required or not, it is well to know that, when burial or cremation will be delayed for a few days, the body can be refrigerated instead of being embalmed. Not all funeral homes have refrigerated storage, but most hospitals do. Another alternative is dry ice. Check the Yellow Pages for a source of dry ice.

In its 1984 funeral rule, the Federal Trade Commission prohibited funeral directors from embalming for a fee unless "state or local law requires embalming" or "prior approval for embalming" has been obtained from the family. But, through misleading ploys, the funeral industry has frequently led people to believe that embalming was a legal requirement, even in the case of cremations. This misrepresentation persists down to the present day.

In order to make more money, some funeral homes will tell you that it is their policy not to permit open-casket viewing, unless the person has first been embalmed. Yet there is no state law that says the body must be embalmed and restored to a lifelike condition for such an observance. Indeed, outside of the United States, embalming is rarely done.

Quite unlike medical embalming done in research laboratories, normal funeral-type embalming is something of a haphazard affair, and is only useful for a few days. In one instance, for example, a 21-year-old accidentally died of an overdose of prescription drugs. He was embalmed on Saturday, and there were visitations for this devastated family throughout Sunday, Monday, and half of Tuesday. But, by Monday, the odor began; and, by Wednesday while arranging for burial in the next state, it become unbearable.

Interestingly enough, embalmers breathe so many toxic fumes while working that, according to CDC reports, they have a higher death rate than the national average.

In his book, *It's Your Funeral,* William L. Coleman explains that "the science of embalming had largely been abandoned for 1,500 years." When it suddenly reemerged in the late 19th century, considerable controversy was aroused. Coleman writes: "Both Christians and humanitarians often objected strenuously. They had visions of bodies being severely mutilated [which embalming somewhat requires]. Ministers denounced it as a desecration of the 'temple of God.' "

The belief that embalming prevents the spread of disease is still widely held, but this has been refuted by several medical authorities. Disease does not run rampant in countries where bodies are seldom embalmed. Studies show that embalming does not affect certain bacteria or viruses. Tuberculosis, smallpox, anthrax, tetanus, and AIDS have all been found in embalmed bodies shortly after death. For more on this, see the Consumer Reports' book, *Funerals: Consumers' Last Rites*. However, in nine states, statutes still require embalming of people who die of specific diseases.

Although embalming was rarely done in early America, it was almost mandatory for some relative to stay by the embalmer's side and witness the procedure. But methods have changed and no one is permitted to be present when the embalming takes place, except apprentices. Indeed, the funeral industry has arranged that everyone is barred by law from being in the embalming room.

If people knew what happens when a person is embalmed, they would not be likely to pay for this procedure, which they are charged for.

The embalming procedure. You may want to skip the next few paragraphs, and go to the section about flowers.

The body is laid out in the undertaker's morgue (today called "the preparation room"). The embalmer has received a nine- or twelve-month post-high school course at an embalming school. The room is filled with fluids, sprays, pastes, oils, powders, creams—to fix or soften tissue, shrink or distend it, dry or restore moisture. There are cosmetics; waxes; paints; and even plaster of Paris, to replace limbs.

But first the blood is removed as quickly as possible from the veins. Then formaldehyde is pumped in through the arteries.

Embalming textbooks recommend that the embalming should take place as soon as possible, even before "cellular death" has occurred. In the average case, this would mean "within an hour after somatic death." "Speaking of fears entertained in the early days of premature burial, one of the effects of embalming by chemical injection, however, has been to dispel fears of live burial." How true; once the blood is removed, chances of live burial are very unlikely. (For more on this, see the textbook, *Principles and Practices of Embalming*).

Although funeral directors will frequently tell you that embalming is required by law, you should be aware of the fact that no law requires embalming, except in cases of certain diseases; no religious doctrine commends it; nor is it dictated by considerations of health or sanitation. In no part of the world, except North America, is it widely used.

Why then do undertakers want to embalm the body? So they can display it in an open, and very expensive, casket. In short, it helps them sell expensive caskets.

By now the fact may be dawning on you that the funeral director intends to embalm your loved one and charge you for it, if at all possible. If you hesitate, he will tell you the law requires it. If you still refuse, he is likely to do it anyway and, frequently, charge you for it as part of his general "services" fee.

Yet, in most states, the signature of next of kin must be obtained before an autopsy may be performed, before the deceased may be cremated, before the body may be turned over to a medical school for research purposes; or such provision must have been made in the deceased person's will for any of that to be done with his remains. Embalming is not, as funeral providers habitually claim, a legal requirement even when the body of the deceased is to be on display in an open casket.

After the blood is removed, between three and

six gallons of a dyed and perfumed solution of form-aldehyde, glycerin, borax, phenol, alcohol, and water is injected; the next step, in the embalming process, is the spearing.

A trocar (a long, hollow needle attached to a tube) is jabbed into the abdomen, near the naval, and jerked around and poked here and there at random around the entrails and chest cavity—the insides of the entire trunk area. The objective is to punch holes in everything in the chest and trunk cavity. The contents are then pumped out and replaced with "cavity fluid." Up to this point, the process has taken about one hour. (When the author learned about this paragraph, he decided he did not want to be embalmed.)

Next comes the sculpting and cosmetics work, to make the body look more attractive.

Eventually, the deceased is wheeled into the viewing room for the mourners to see during viewing hours.

Obviously, if an open casket viewing is not requested by the next of kin, then there is no need for the cosmetic work.

For your information, open casket viewings were not done in Bible times, or later in history,—until fairly modern times. Over 68% of all American funerals in the mid-1990s featured an open casket. Yet this is a custom unknown in other parts of the world. Foreigners are astonished that Americans do this.

Flowers. The funeral director wants you to sign up, for him to provide flowers. Funeral flowers accounted for 65%-70% of the cut-flower industry's revenue in 1960, and many funeral homes either had an ownership interest or a commission "arrangement" with the local florist. By 1970, the market share had dropped to 40%; and it has, according to trade sources, gone down steadily since then. By 1995, sales had further declined to 14% of what was a $15 billion florist industry (up from $414 million in 1960).

You do not have to accede to the funeral salesman's urging that you sign up for them to provide flowers. You can either just have a few friends bring flowers from their gardens (that is the way it is done in rural England) or you can request that money be donated to charity instead of being spent on flowers.

A survey of newspaper obituary (death) notices reveals that 50% to 75% contain requests such as "Donations to (charity) preferred." But some newspapers refuse to print that sentence in their notices.

Clergy. Unfortunately, it should also be mentioned that some ministers in urban areas, who frequently conduct funerals, make deals with local funeral directors. They gently direct relatives of dead parishioners to certain morticians who, in turn, pay them a percentage of the casket or the entire funeral.

We live in a strange world today. People want your money so much they arrange to kill your unborn child, they feed you foodless food and diseased meat; and, when you become sick from it all, they take your money at the hospitals and, finally, at the funeral home.

Monuments. Above-ground monuments (in earlier centuries called "tombstones") come in a variety of sizes and shapes. They may be quite small—perhaps only four inches square—made of granite, marble, or bronze, installed flat on the ground, and cost as little as $200 or $300. Or they can be as large as 30 inches wide by 72 inches long. Called "ledgers," they lie flat on the grave and cost about $6,000. Others can be larger. Vertical pieces, including statuary, can cost as much as $100,000 or more.

Other items and services. There is more than caskets, vaults, and monuments that the funeral home wants to sell you. There are also various transportation expenses, undertaker's "services," clergy honorarium, graveside services, and more cemetery fees. More on cemeteries soon.

Funeral directors offer to sell you "burial clothing" for your deceased. But it is of lower quality and is often open in the back. Most people are buried in their own clothes.

You may also be offered marked-up stationery, such as guest registers, announcement cards, prayer cards, thank you cards, and acknowledgment notes. These can be purchased at a stationery store for less.

You may need the funeral home hearse to transport the heavy casket to the cemetery, but there is no need for any other funeral home vehicles! You will be charged for extra vehicles unless you specify that only the hearse is to be used.

You can also decide not to have flowers at the graveside service, but you may still be charged for the removal and disposal of any other flowers which are brought there; so have a friend remove them as soon as the graveside service is ended.

Instead of the funeral director's professional pall-bearers, recruit your own friends to bear the casket.

The funeral director may offer to tape or video the funeral service for you. If you want it done, ask a friend to do it.

You can have a friend send in an obituary notice to the local newspaper instead of having the funeral home charge you for the service. But big city newspapers only include obituaries of well-known people. More on obituaries later in the section on by-passing the funeral industry.

Death certificates are more complicated, and you do best to let the funeral director fill it out. However, later in this book we tell you exactly how to do it yourself!

Let the funeral director fill out the burial permit.

Federal regulations prohibit the funeral director from profiting from expenditures for flowers, newspaper notices, clergy honoraria, etc.; but, it is often included under the "basic services" charge. You should know what is happening.

You can save a variety of funeral home charges (visitation room, chapel, flower stands, lighting, etc.) by having the funeral service in a church or synagogue and only paying for the costs of preparing and transporting the body.

Viewing vs. visitation. Viewing occurs when the mourners view the deceased. This can be done at the hospital, prior to the funeral. Or it can be done at an open casket viewing (which you will pay for).

Visitation occurs when the family gathers to-gether, informally, to reminisce over the past. The casket is either closed or not there at all. Visitation can take place anywhere. It is a wonderful healing process for all. For many, it is more comfortable than an open casket viewing. There is encouragement and comfort in the spontaneous sharing of memories.

FUNERAL PRICES

Summarized prices. It would be well to pro-vide you with an overview of typical funeral prices. These are average costs for funerals and may vary in your community. Because they come from vari-ous sources and dates, the prices will vary.

Funeral home charges are, today, eight to ten times what they were thirty years ago. Cemetery prices have increased just as much. But in this sec-tion, we will only discuss typical funeral home costs, as they are, today, at about the end of the 20th cen-tury.

By federal law (established by the Federal Trade Commission, FTC), you must be given a General Price List (GPL), a casket price list, and an outer burial container price list when you inquire about arrangements and prices. You may keep a copy of the GPL. You must also be given an itemized state-ment of your final choices when contracting for a funeral.

You will want to make sure the contract only includes those items you have selected. Take the time to get a total amount written down in ink. Be sure to sign the contract, even if you were not asked to do so. This is a protection you may need later. The funeral industry sometimes adds additional costs later on (especially in "pre-need" contracts; more on that trap later in this book).

The FTC permits a "nondeclinable" fee for "basic services of staff." ("Nondeclinable" means you cannot get the price lowered.) If you have a funeral home or other mortuary establishment care for your loved one, you must pay this fee, in addition to the cost of specific funeral goods and services you select.

Yet you get almost nothing for this fee. It includes the time the funeral director sells you his service, the time it takes to make arrangements if the body is shipped out of the area, the time needed to request required permits, the time needed for you to fill out the death certificate, and the faxing or mailing of the obituary (which you wrote) to the newspaper.

Some funeral homes set a high nondeclinable fee, others a lower one. Generally, those who set a lower fee charge more for their caskets and other charges.

Here is the simplest way to reduce your costs:

1 - Conduct the funeral yourself (more on this later).

2 - Have a simple (simple) cremation rather than a funeral.

3 - Have a "memorial service," perhaps in your church or home instead of a funeral in the funeral home. If you select this, shop around and find a funeral home with a low basic charge for their fu-

nerals. Remember that, by FTC regulations, they are required to give you such information.

One estimated average. According to the funeral industry's own figures, the average undertaker's bill, which was $750 in 1961 for casket and "services,"—is now over $7,000, to which must be added the cost of a burial vault, flowers, clothing, clergy and musician's honorarium, and cemetery charges. When these are all added up, the total average cost for an adult's funeral today is over $7,800.

The price of vaults can be as expensive and fancy as caskets, with some prices going as high as $7,000 or more.

The national average for embalming is $350. The price depends on the amount of restoration that is needed or requested. There might be an additional $150 charge for autopsied bodies.

NFDA's averages. In recent years, the National Funeral Directors Association (NFDA) and other trade associations have provided their members with annual estimates of "average prices" currently charged for mortuary services and vaults. The estimates of the NFDA and FFDA (Federated Funeral Directors of America) vary only a little. FFDA's average for 1995 was $4,211 for "services plus casket," plus $770 for outside container (the vault). Industry observers have no doubt that the dissemination of these numbers within the trade serves to establish uniform price minimums.

IFIC data. In 1982, Henry Wasielewski, a Catholic priest in Phoenix, Arizona, organized the Interfaith Funeral Information Committee (IFIC). The IFIC has carried on a campaign of finding out funeral and burial costs. It is staffed by volunteer clergy from several denominations, social workers, and community leaders. (Later in this book, we will tell you how to contact IFIC.)

Sample: Houston price range. Here are some IFIC price guidelines in the mid-1990s; that is, mid-range prices which it considers to be acceptable, for example, in the Houston, Texas, area:

A retail casket price of $428 to $600, metal, with a choice of three colors. (The wholesale cost is $285, a markup of 50% to 100% of what the IFIC considers reasonable.)

A reasonable service charge for a "traditional" funeral: $800 to $1,400.

A reasonable price range for a complete funeral—including metal casket, choice of colors, embalming, and viewing: $1,450 to $2,500.

In the Houston area, 16 mortuaries provide a complete funeral for the recommended maximum of $2,500 or less. Another 97 charge $3,000 to $9,910. The casket markup for some of them is more than five times the wholesale cost.

Seven establishments had the highest total funeral costs: $7,020 to $9,910. Interestingly enough, all of them are owned by the giant conglomerate Service Corporation International (SCI)—the largest chain-owned funeral business in the world. We will discuss this funeral industry giant later in this book.

One of the first things you want to find out is whether the funeral home you are speaking with is home-owned or part of a chain. Unfortunately, if it is part of a chain, they may tell you it is locally owned.

Sample: mid-range Washington, D.C. price list. This list will enlighten you as to thirteen different items you could be charged for by a funeral home. (But some will include additional charges for filling out forms, faxing, etc.)

This was the Pumphrey Funeral Home, Washington, D.C., general price list for several years ago:

Basic services of funeral director and staff $1,525 / Transfer of remains to the funeral home $255 / Embalming $370—or—no embalming (refrigeration) $375 / Dressing, cosmetics, casketing $215 / Use of facilities for viewing, per day $290 / Use of facilities for funeral ceremony $315 / Hearse $235 / Flower car $85 / Sedan $115 / Limo $120 / Total for services and use of premises $3,375.

Funeral homes must think the public is made of money! Notice that the charge is about the same amount, whether or not embalming is done.

To the above prices, must be added the cost of the casket (quoted as between $500 to $25,000; the cheapest steel casket was $2,000); the cost of the outside burial container, or vault (required now by almost all cemeteries), is $525 to $6,500.

The IFIC found that the Pumphrey Funeral Home was average and its prices fell in the "middle range," nationwide.

Lisa Carlson, in her book, *Caring for the Dead: Your Final Act of Love*, came across a Swanton, Vermont, widow whose mother's funeral in 1993 cost $2,900. When her father died in June 1995, the identical funeral at the same funeral home was billed at $7,100. The widow who trusted that the funeral home would provide the same service for about the same cost was betrayed. She had signed on the dotted line without noticing the price (perhaps before it was typed in).

Sample: Houston add-ons. Most people will be talked into more than just the above-listed basics. Here they are:

Use of facilities and staff services for visitation (per day) $98 / Funeral service in the chapel $725—or—Staff and services in other facility $725—or—Chapel for memorial service without remains present $725 / Equipment and staff services at graveside $515 / Additional charge for use of facilities and staff on Sunday or holiday $600 / Caskets $2,598 to $25,145 / Copper vault ("resists the entrance of outside elements") $20,378.

The $98, listed above, is the charge you will pay each time you want to stop by and visit the crypt, where you loved one is located in the mausoleum! Personally, I would rather have a loved one buried where I do not have to pay to visit the grave.

Sample: Denver. The consolidators (large firms which own many local funeral homes and cemeteries) charge the most for caskets. For example, in a Denver funeral home, fronting for SCI (Service Corporation International), an extremely cheap and unimpressive gray-cloth-covered casket is retailed to its customers for $1,995. The standard wholesale cost of this box is $140. SCI's cost is even lower because of its volume discounts.

Amount of Casket Markup. The IFIC publishes

an annual report on wholesale versus retail prices of funeral goods. The Batesville Casket Company claims to be the largest casket manufacturer in the world. In its 1995 report, the IFIC revealed typical profit margins on these caskets.

The *Autumn Oak* casket, constructed of solid oak and wholesaled for $880, was sold by funeral homes for $2,200 to $3,080 and, sometimes, $4,840.

The firm's *India Star* silver model, in 16-gauge steel and wholesaled for $1,220, was regularly sold for $3,050 to $3,660 or up to $4,880.

The September/October 1995 issue of *Consumers Digest* surveyed the wholesale and retail price sheets it obtained from major casket manufacturers: Here are a few of its findings:

Cloth-covered particle board: W (wholesale): $167, R (Retail): $500, P (profit): 199%.

Solid pine: W: $749, R: $1,897, P: 153%.

Solid oak: W: $801, R: $2,600, P: 224%.

16 gauge steel: W: $1,074, R: $2,255, P: 109%.

Solid cheery: W: $1,284, R: $3,550, P: 176%.

Stainless steel: W: $989, R: $4,050, P: 309%.

Solid mahogany: W: $1,810, R: $8,500, P: 369%.

Bronze (48 oz.): W: $8,725, R: $31,000, P: 732%.

Copper (solid): W: $1,625, R: $33,000, P: 1930%.

Consumer Reports noted that the conglomerate-owned funeral homes regularly purchase those caskets for 25% less than wholesale. Yet, as you will learn in a later chapter, they generally charge more for their funerals.

2 – FACTS ABOUT CEMETERIES AND MAUSOLEUMS

Burial plots. You thought you paid everything when you stopped by the funeral home. But there is also the cemetery. In America, there is an ongoing rivalry between the funeral homes and the larger cemeteries. Both want to contact the customer first and get in on the ground floor of his money supply, before it runs out. The funeral home generally has the advantage; but, in the urban areas, the cemeteries are sending salesmen out to sell "advance-payment" burial plots. The larger cemeteries / mausoleums are in direct competition with the funeral homes.

You should also be aware of how they handle their "immediate need" sales. These occur when someone dies and the survivors need to pay for a funeral and burial. The first thing the cemetery wants is to insist that the family make a personal visit to the cemetery and not permit the purchase of the grave to be handled through the funeral director. Some even refuse to make a sale over the phone in an "at-need" (immediate need) situation. They want the lion's share in the sale of the casket and burial plot.

Other cemetery services. The family visit to the cemetery also provides opportunity to describe other cemetery services to the grieving one, such as bronze memorials (*i.e.*, an expensive gravestone), flowers, mausoleum crypts, and cremation facilities.

If you only purchase a plot, they will repeatedly contact you "through a carefully planned program, to provide counsel and assistance for lot owners," until you also buy a "memorial." They are persistent.

Would you like an example of how this is done? First a letter is sent to the family, announcing that the Cedar Park memorial counselor and director of the Family Counseling Service will call upon them shortly, "to secure the information necessary for the Historical Record and present you with a photographic record of the services at Cedar Memorial." Three days later, the counselor arrives at the home and "suggests the purchase of a bronze memorial." In the middle of the month following the service, the counselor is after the family again—this time to invite them to a "counseling program" at the cemetery chapel. That in turn is followed up by yet another personal visit. If all else fails, "Dr. Dill always visits them if a memorial has not been selected."

Another trick of the cemeteries is to make it difficult for competitive vault and monument companies to sell their products. The cemeteries may charge an arbitrary toll for use of their roads in connection with vault installations by outside firms. They may require that all vaults be installed by cemetery personnel. They may not permit monument (gravestones) makers to install them, insisting that only cemetery personnel are permitted to do the job.

Many (if not most) memorial gardens (cemeteries) are "nonprofit." The acreage is owned by a sister for-profit corporation. The profit is split, but the gardens bear all the expense; so it always remains "nonprofit" while the owners happily lug their money to the bank.

Opening and closing the grave. This is an additional expense. A backhoe operator can open a grave in less than 30 minutes and close it in even less time. The average cost to cemetery operators in the U.S. for digging and filling a grave is $50 to $75, depending on soil conditions. But the customer is charged $300 to $700. Some East Coast cemeteries charge as much as $1,500. If the grave is opened or closed on evenings, weekends, or holidays, the cost will be double overtime. At the request of cemetery associations, a number of states have enacted laws, making it illegal for anyone but the cemetery to open and close the grave.

Procedure at the grave. A grave is not six feet deep, as commonly thought. Most graves are four to five feet deep, three and one-half feet wide, and eight feet long. By the time the cover to the liner or vault is in place, there is only about 12 to 18 inches of dirt above it.

The dirt that is removed is either trucked away from the site or left nearby and covered with a blanket of artificial grass.

After the mourners leave, the casket is lowered into the grave; the liner or vault lid is placed securely in place; and either the gravediggers, or more often a backhoe, puts the dirt back into the grave, compacting it, to help prevent any settling of the earth. The pneumatic-powered soil tamping equipment frequently cracks the lid and seals of the vault, rendering them almost immediately useless for the purpose of protecting the casketed body and grave. Soon rainwater enters and soaks everything.

Perpetual care. This may be arranged by the payment of a lump sum or may be included in the sale price of the cemetery lot. In earlier decades, cemeteries billed families annually for the upkeep of grave sites. In reality, the grass is generally mowed everywhere in the graveyard, including those graves which no longer include perpetual care. By the way, perpetual care does not include the grave marker. In most instances, that is covered by the person's homeowner's insurance policy.

"Abandoned" grave lots. Here is information you should know, in case you buy a cemetery lot ahead of time. Many states have provisions permitting a cemetery to declare burial plots "abandoned" if unused after 50 years or so. So if you purchase a plot and do not use it within half a century, the cemetery will later resell it. If you have paid for a cemetery lot, and the years are passing, you might want to send a note to the cemetery every so often, so they will know you have not forgotten them.

Read the fine print. Whenever you buy a cemetery lot, you are agreeing to abide by the cemetery's regulations. So be sure and read the fine print on the agreement before you sign it.

CEMETERY
AND MAUSOLEUM FEES

Acreage costs. Let us compare how much is made on acreage: Subdividing land for people to live on only yields six homes (50-by-100-foot lots) per acre. In contrast, an old-fashioned cemetery packs in 1,500 or more "lots," each one 8 feet by 3 feet.

But the modern "lawn-type" cemetery, with flat bronze markers, set flush in the ground, produces 7-by-3-foot graves and makes mowing easy with giant mowers. This saves 75% of the maintenance cost. These new cemeteries, pioneered by Forest Lawn in Glendale, California, contain 1,815 adult graves per acre.

Double-depth graves are also sold, with husband and wife graves on top of one another. "Babyland" graves (graves for infants) fit three in the space occupied by one adult.

But mausoleums make the most money per acre.

Facts about mausoleums. A mausoleum is a building which has "crypts" (another name for coffins) slid into openings in its walls. A mausoleum will provide you with a complete funeral, followed by placement of the crypt (by sliding) into a wall space you have purchased.

The latest trend is the community mausoleum. This is the best moneymaker of all! Here is how it works: With little or no cash, the company acquires an option on some rural acreage and has it zoned for cemetery use. He then purchases landscaping plans and begins selling "pre-need" crypts through squads of telemarketers seeking an invitation to make home calls. After about a third of the crypts are sold, the entire building has been paid for and the mausoleum is built of low-cost concrete blocks. A rectangular building, it has steel crypt spaces set in the inside walls on both sides of each aisle. Light enters overhead through skylights which cover the ceiling. Steel boxes ("crypts") are pushed into the spaces for the "eternal rest" of the occupants. (The size of each crypt is generally 32 inches wide, 25 inches high, and 90 inches long.)

With seven crypts high, plus long corridors, a very large number of crypts can be accommodated. The potential gross sale is $4,308,000 per acre! The net potential is $2,808,000 per acre.

By the way, many cemeteries and all mausoleums add a 10% to 25% surcharge, if you want "perpetual care." You thought you had already paid for that!

Average cemetery fees. As mentioned earlier, the cemetery may be partly owned or wholly owned by the funeral home, or they may have a secret agreement. But they may also be in direct competition for your business. Therefore, the cemetery might charge you anywhere from $500 to $2,500, for a cemetery plot, or they may add on charges because you did not purchase the vault or memorial stone from them.

The price of a single lot in a small-town cemetery can be as low as $100, including perpetual care. Large commercial cemeteries, however, are likely to charge several thousand dollars for a single lot. With the sale of "pre-need" lots, many cemeteries are able to make so much money that they are being bought up by the consolidators and other big corporations. (More on this under *Consolidators* and *Pre-need*.)

Sample: Houston basic crypt. This is a bottom price for a funeral, followed by placement of the coffin ("crypt") in the same firm's mausoleum in the Houston, Texas, area.

"Minimum Services" $1,682 / Transportation of body from place of death to funeral home $355 / Refrigeration or embalming $425 / Minimum sealed (gasketed) casket $2,598 / Transferring body from funeral home to crypt $275 / Removing and replacing the faceplate $660 / Vehicle for picking up permits $100 / Total $6,095.

The $275 charge at this funeral home was for the laborious task of taking the body 200 yards from the funeral home to the crypt. They charge $100 to provide a vehicle to go to the courthouse.

For your information, the cemeteries in North America that yield the highest profit returns are those like Forest Lawn in Glendale, California, which have self-contained mortuaries, with their own funeral establishments, flower shops, and large burial plot and / or crypt areas.

3 – WHAT ABOUT CREMATION?

ALL ABOUT CREMATION

Cremation is the process by which the deceased is burned and his ashes are placed in a container of some kind.

The ashes are then buried, scattered over the sea or land, or kept in an urn. The cemetery prefers that you pay for a small, but very expensive metal container, called an urn, which is then placed for permanent storage ("perpetual care") in a niche, in a building called a columbarium.

There were 41 cremations in the United States in 1841. The total had risen to 13,281 a year by the end of the century. In 1900, there were 26 crematories (places where cremations are done) in America; by 1980 there were 585, and the number is rapidly increasing. At the present time, 22% of deaths end in cremation. It is estimated that, by 2010, the number may increase over 40%.

Boxes for cremation. Simple, economical cremation containers include pine, plywood, pressboard, or heavy cardboard. The lowest-cost containers are generally labeled as "alternative containers," the expression used in the FTC's Funeral Rule. As mentioned elsewhere, it is possible to rent a casket for viewing.

Cremation in a casket. In order to make extra money, funeral directors will frequently recommend that, prior to cremation, the deceased be placed in a metal casket. Loved ones are often talked into doing this. Yet this, frankly, is a ridiculous procedure. The only gain is extra cash in the pocket of the funeral home director.

Crematories, whose equipment is designed for the combustion of wood or other soft material, are not able to deal with burning up metal coffins!

Lightweight metal caskets are burned longer than normal, in order to buckle and melt them. Instead of the ashes of the bones remaining, the fire was so hot that hardly anything remains except melted metal!

If a heavy, more expensive, casket is ordered by the customer: When it arrives at the crematory, the workers know that it will be impossible to melt it down—so the body is removed and cremated. But this leaves a problem as to what to do with the casket. State law forbids using it again, and the family would sue if they found it afterward in the city dump. So the workers at the crematory have to smash it to pieces and then sell it for scrap.

The cremation process. The cremation chamber is lined with fire brick, able to withstand heat up to 3,500° F. The cremation process usually occurs at 1,800° F. If the chamber is already hot from a previous cremation, the temperature may reach 2,400° F. Natural gas or fuel oil generally fires the unit, but propane or electricity is sometimes used. Burners are installed along the sides and top; some new models also have them underneath. Cremation time is generally completed in one or two hours, but some units require two to three hours. Many have automatic shut-offs.

When the cremation is complete, the chamber must cool down. Then the door is opened and about three to seven pounds of clean, white bone fragments are removed.

The staff is very careful to remove every particle of the cremains. They are then placed on a metal tray, where a magnet is used to remove all metal. (Keep in mind that the person was cremated in clothes which may have contained some metal.)

The fragments are then placed in a pulverizer which reduces them to small bits and powder. The remains may be more gray than white, depending on the amount of heat that was used. The cremains are then placed in temporary containers, usually of tin, plastic, or cardboard, and shipped inside another box by registered mail. (UPS will not knowingly ship them; in some places Fed Express or Purolator Courier may be used.) The cremains are usually sent to the local funeral director. But, if you arranged for the funeral without the help of a funeral home, they would be shipped directly to you.

Your right to keep the ashes. Crematories won a legal victory in California, when they got the state legislature to enact a law forbidding the scattering of the ashes, by private parties, anywhere. But, what the funeral homes do not want the survivors to know is that they still have the right to simply take the ashes home with them. The laws of every state permit the ownership of the ashes of a cremated person. What they do with them thereafter is up to them. They may wish to bury the ashes.

When no other arrangement has been made by the survivors, the ashes must be handed over to them.

Your right to scatter the ashes. In all states but California, cremains may be scattered if they are converted to unrecognizable skeletal remains. (Not all crematories provide the pulverizing of the remains to small bits and particles; so, if scattering is planned, you will want to confirm that the crematory will pulverize the remains.)

Another problem in California concerns a rule which permits the funeral homes to require you to fill out a cremation form supplied by them. In order to obtain a copy, you must pay a large amount for it!

Scattering vs. burial. You have the right to bury the ashes or, in every state except California, to scatter them. But there are advantages to burying them. They are then in a single location. At the urging of friends, one mother had agreed to ocean scattering because her teenage son had loved surfing. At the time, it seemed appropriate. But a year or so later, she felt an emptiness for not having a "place" by which to remember her son. The cremains can be kept at home; buried privately; or, if you wish, scattered in a flower garden; etc. In all of these ways, you know where the remains are located.

If the cremains are buried in a tight container, in case you move to a distant place, you can, if you wish, dig up the container and take it with you.

Making extra on cremations. For several decades, funeral directors tried to dissuade people from cremation. But eventually they changed tactics; and now they encourage a complete funeral ceremony, concluded by the burial of the ashes in a cemetery or placement in a niche.

An alternate method is to talk customers into purchasing a fancy urn. This is a metal container to hold the ashes.

"During a 1997 *'Keys to Cremation Success'* symposium sponsored by the *Funeral Service Insider,* one presentation was called *'How to Add $1,400 or More to Each Cremation Call.'* The presenter told his audience that 'seeing Mom in a cardboard box sometimes prompts a family member to ask if we don't have something a little nicer.' A similar suggestion was put forward by the *Funeral Service Insider:* 'When families don't buy an urn, require them to purchase a temporary container to hold the cremains. But make sure you label (or stamp) that box with the words 'temporary container' on all four sides . . That makes families most likely to upgrade beyond the temporary container.' "

The latest device used by some cemeteries is the requirement of an "urn vault." This is an outer container, in which the urn, destined to be buried, must be placed. This is another method to separate you from your money.

Direct cremation firms. In the early 1970s, firms offering "direct cremation" came on the scene. These firms offered a simple cremation for a fixed fee of around $255, roughly linked to the Social Security death benefit. For an additional $250, the ashes would be scattered at sea from a plane or boat.

Having gotten the California legislature to ban the private scattering or burial of the ashes (even though the law cannot be enforced), sometimes the ashes are just dumped by a large cremation firm. In that way, they can avoid the extra expense (for which they were handsomely paid) of putting the ashes where they contracted to scatter them. For example, in 1997, 5,200 boxes of cremated remains were stored instead of being dumped at sea.

Investigation has repeatedly disclosed that the majority of survivors, who paid to have the ashes scattered, are never told that they can take the ashes home with them.

The advantage of "direct cremation" is that you by-pass the funeral home. But, even if you do that, it is best if you have the cremains shipped directly to you rather than being scattered. In this way you will be certain that they are placed where you want them.

The consolidators. We will discuss these large conglomerate funeral organizations later. Even more than the home-owned funeral homes, the consolidators are likely to tell you that you cannot have the cremains or do with them as you wish.

Here is part of a sales script, used with cremation customers by one of the consolidators (SCI), to get them to place the cremains permanently in an expensive company-owned location:

"Memorization creates an opportunity for family and friends to say good-bye in a dignified manner. It provides a link to the past, future and present by allowing generations of loved ones a permanent place to go to reflect and remember. And most importantly, it provides a time and place for you and yours to go to heal and provide closure. There are specific laws and guidelines that pertain to what can be done with the cremated human remains.

"Almost all urns can be buried. Burial can take place in a family plot or urn garden [both in the company-owned cemetery]. There are specific laws on where you can bury cremated remains."

But the last sentence in each paragraph is not true; the exception is California, which does not permit private scattering of cremains. They may be placed anywhere or kept at home.

In reality, there are no "cremains police" in California, so the remains can be placed anywhere there as well.

The Neptune Society. The Neptune Society got in on the ground floor of this new way to make money. Founded in Los Angeles in the 1970s, it is now "the largest direct cremation firm in the world," with offices in large cities in California, New York, and Florida.

By taking the name, "Society," Neptune gives the impression that it is one of the nonprofit funeral and memorial societies which have built invaluable goodwill by their consumer protection activities. (More on the societies later in this book.)

Neptune advertises heavily and offers to provide you with a low-cost cremation. Sounds great, but there are problems. Like all big companies, Neptune sometimes cuts corners in order to maximize profits.

First, its low-cost cremation is now $1,599.00. (That is the current price. In preparation for this book, I personally phoned them.) There are funeral homes which have lower prices. While briefly shopping around, I found I could obtain a cremation from one local funeral home for $1,200. Another funeral home said that, if I would purchase in advance, with all the money going into a trust (but will it? more on that later), I would be given a $750 cremation. So you want to shop around.

Second, Neptune has been involved in lawsuits. For example, in the mid-1980s, Neptune settled a class action lawsuit involving 300 families for $22 million, plus $5 million court costs.

In 1988, ashes of 5,342 corpses were discovered in a remote mountain location by a passing pilot.

In 1988, an out-of-court settlement against Neptune was made for $12.7 million.

A 1991 class action suit, for purportedly mishandling and commingling thousands of corpses, was recently settled for $6.8 million.

In the mid-1990s, three Neptune crematories, without admitting guilt, agreed to financial audits and to reimburse the state for its investigation.

The uncomposed, badly decomposed body of a former mayor of Burbank, California, was discovered after four and a half months in a refrigerator; the case was settled for over $1 million.

The original Neptune price for a cremation in the 1970s was $255. By 1996, it was $1,200; today it is $1,599. In addition, by the 1990s, added charges were tacked on for "sea scattering without family or friends present," $125; add $395 for family groups of up to eight; add $295 for "witnessing the beginning of the cremation process."

When I spoke with a representative of Neptune

on the phone, he told me I had to be a California resident. I mentioned that I had a son living there; he quickly replied that would be good enough.

CREMATION FEES

Denver. Twenty funeral homes in the Denver area will provide direct cremations for less than $700, cremation container and crematory fee included. The funeral homes owned by SCI and Loewen quote prices of $2,745 to $3,985 for the identical service. So it pays to shop around.

One SCI price: Here is the price list of cremation by one SCI funeral home: "Minimum Services" for direct cremation $1,252 / Transportation of the body from place of death $355 / Refrigeration $425 / Cardboard box $275 / Crematory charge $475 / Vehicle for picking up certificates $100 / Total $2,882.

Neptune. In the mid-1990s, the California Department of Consumer Affairs (CDCA) noted that, of $12.6 million for cremations by three Neptune outlets, $9 million was allegedly for the sale of caskets and urns.

Yet neither caskets nor urns are required by law. A *Dateline NBC* broadcast showed a tape of a Neptune salesman explaining that the law requires a casket (cost $400) for cremation. Yet CDCA found that all Neptune bodies were cremated in a shroud.

The Neptune salesman also said that, if a casket is not used, a metal urn is required by law (cost $75); whereas a $2 cardboard box is actually used during the cremation.

The present writer wonders whether the paid-for caskets and urns are just put back into stock.

Urn prices: wholesale and retail. The wholesale price range for the "art-urn line," by the Batesville Casket Company (which calls itself the "world's largest" casket and urn company), is $70 to $575. These urns are then sold to the customer for $50 to $1,695.

Rented caskets. A 1995 report, by the Cremation Association of North America (CANA), stated that 18% of the cremations were done uncoffined and 28% involved the use of a rented casket (which was not then burned up). The rental cost varies from $600 to $800 for the one or two days' occupancy. The rented caskets (with removable interiors, costing the funeral home less than $100) are reused over and over again. But the industry is phasing out the rental business because it claims it generates insufficient profit. The average price charged for "cremation caskets" is $1,298 to $3,000. (After writing this paragraph, it has been discovered that the latest trend is for funeral homes to avoid renting caskets; they make far more selling even their cheapest caskets.)

SHOULD YOU CONSIDER CREMATION?

No one can decide such a question for another. But here are several thoughts to consider.

The cost factor. Over the past half century, there has been a tremendous increase in the number of cremations. There appears to be a corollary between the spiraling rise in funeral and burial costs and the number of people who, in disgust, are turning to the lower-cost cremation.

What is the principle here? Is it what happens to the body after death? Both burial and cremation accomplish the same objective. But there is also the cost principle. Would God have us spend an excessive amount of money on funerals, forced on us at exorbitant prices, or would He prefer that we do it at far less expense? That is a matter for each to decide for himself.

Fortunately, later in this book we will explain how you may be able to bury (not cremate) your loved one (or have yourself buried)—and by-pass the funeral home entirely. That is a way to reduce the cost factor even more than cremation can accomplish.

In England, 72% of the dead are cremated. The average crematory charge of $80 includes the use of a chapel, not usually available in North American cremations. The body is laid in a simple, wooden coffin that is not painted or varnished. In England, about 90% of the cremated remains are then scattered (or "strewn," as they call it there). Sometimes they are scattered over the sea or the countryside, but more often in a "Garden of Remembrance." This is consecrated ground, set aside for that purpose. Sometimes there is a nominal charge for the scattering service, if the garden is part of a crematorium or cemetery.

Other factors to consider. During the winter months when the ground is frozen, immediate cremation may be preferable to waiting for a spring earth burial.

In addition, it is not uncommon for a person to die— far away from the planned final resting place. Some 8,000 Americans die abroad each year. When the remains must be transported over a great distance, cremation may be a convenient and desirable choice.

Cautions about cremation. The funeral industry controls the cremation procedure; you cannot avoid the funeral industry, as you can with a burial. Even though, by selecting a cremation, you avoided an expensive funeral, they are going to charge you all they can for a cremation. It can easily run $1500 to $2500 for a procedure which is relatively simple. However, if you shop around—especially in advance when you have more time to carefully consider such matters,—you may be able to locate a firm which will do it for $700.

Another fact, to be aware of, is that the funeral home may try to sell you a casket for the cremation or an equally expensive urn.

Part of the cost is due to the fact that the body is taken to a larger city, where the cremation is done, and the ashes are then returned to you.

The cost of moving the body of a loved one from one place to another is quite expensive. It is a cost to be avoided, if possible. In one instance, a person was taken from Knoxville, Tennessee, to a location not far from Chattanooga, and the family was charged $1800 for just that one trip.

A friend who has traveled extensively in Mexico as a missionary has told the present writer that, down there, if a family moves a body from one lo-cality to another, the law requires them to pay 500 pesos to each cemetery they pass! So, in order to avoid that expense, they transport him in a car sit-ting upright between two people.

Another drawback would be if you want all the particles, composing the deceased person, to be buried in the same place. Cremation will carry the soft tissues into the air, where they will eventually land here and there. Only the bone powder will be given to you to bury. So cremation is not a direct burial of your loved one in the ground.

Although the cost of a standard cremation is definitely less than a funeral home-arranged burial, it is still generally high: easily $1,200 to $1,500.

Another problem is your concern that, if you sign a pre-need contract ("guaranteeing" you a lower cremation price), the money which, supposedly has been placed in trust, may be misused. (Read the section on *"Pay-Ahead Contracts,"* later in this book. You will there learn that going through a bank is the safest way to do that.)

Lowest-cost cremations. In summary, the low-est-cost cremations are obtainable by contacting your nearest crematory for a "direct cremation." This by-passes the funeral home and all its expenses. This will cost you several hundred dollars.

An alternative is to donate your body to a medi-cal school, with the proviso that, about two years later, when they are finished studying it, they will cremate and return the ashes to you. (More on this later, in the section on *"Medical Gifts."*)

In summary. Should a person select burial or cremation for himself? This is definitely a matter for individual thought and decision. Financial needs are involved, and so are personal convictions.

Do you want to avoid handing over a lot of money to a funeral home? Are you able to be buried without paying a funeral home to do it? Is cremation your only alternative to a fairly expensive funeral? In a later major section, we will consider how to by-pass the funeral industry entirely, and bury your beloved dead privately.

The Biblical factor. In the 19th century, some clergy objected to cremation, declaring that, if the decomposed body was not in one place, Christ could not resurrect it at the final resurrection.

But many believe, as one writer has suggested, that the Lord is not indebted to pre-existing matter in the resurrection and does not necessarily even use the same particles in the resurrected body. That would be understandable; since, each seven years throughout your life every tissue and atom in your body is changed. There is nothing in your body that was there eight years ago.

In a burial, the body decomposes and eventually turns into dust. In a cremation, the body is turned into dust. It would appear that both fulfill the Biblical command, especially if the cremated ashes are then buried or strewn on the ground. (In contrast, burial in a metal casket turns the body to a miserable soup.)

What does the Bible teach? Whether burial or cremation is used, after death we return to dust:

"Till thou return unto the ground; for out of it wast thou taken; for dust thou art, and unto dust shalt thou return."—*Genesis 3:19*.

"Now shall I sleep in the dust; and thou shalt seek me in the morning, but I shall not be."—*Job 17:21*.

"What profit is there in my blood, when I go down to the pit? Shall the dust praise Thee? Shall it declare Thy truth?"—*Psalm 30:9*.

"He remembereth that we are dust. As for man, his days are as grass: as a flower of the field, so he flourisheth. For the wind passeth over it, and it is gone; and the place thereof shall know it no more."—*Psalm 103:14-16*.

"His breath goeth forth, he returneth to his earth; in that very day his thoughts perish."—*Psalm 146:4*.

"And many of them that sleep in the dust of the earth shall awake, some to everlasting life, and some to shame and everlasting contempt."—*Daniel 12:2*.

"All go unto one place; all are of the dust, and all turn to dust again."—*Ecclesiastes 3:20*.

"Then shall the dust return to the earth as it was."—*Ecclesiastes 12:7*.

Cremation in the Bible. Not only burial but cremation was done in the Bible:

"And all the valiant men arose, and went all night, and took the body of Saul and the bodies of his sons from the wall of Bethshan, and came to Jabesh, and burnt them there. And they took their bones, and buried them under a tree at Jabesh."— *1 Samuel 31:12-13*.

That is exactly how a cremation is done. The

body is burned and all the soft tissue turns to dust. The powder, primarily consisting of the bones, is placed in a box and given to one's loved ones. The ashes can be kept in a container in the home, sprinkled on your property, or placed in an expensive crypt provided by the funeral industry.

Jewish burials in the time of Christ. How did the Jews bury their dead in the time of Christ? It was done in a manner which had effects similar to cremation. They would place the body on a stone slab in a family cave, cut out of the rock. About a year later, only the bones would remain, and these would be put in a stone ossuary for permanent storage (*"ossuary"* [also written *"ossuarium"*] means "bone box; *"os"* is an ancient word for "bone."). About seven years ago, Israeli archaeologists found the ossuary of Caiaphas, the high priest who condemned Christ to death. What remained of his bones were inside a stone box with a rounded lid, which had ornate designs and his name engraved into the sides. As his family members died, their bones eventually went into the same box.

---

4 – IF YOU SELECT THE FUNERAL INDUSTRY TO PROVIDE THE CARE

DANGERS IN PAY-AHEAD CONTRACTS

Pay-ahead plans. Pre-need funeral contracts

are frequently one of the most dangerous financial traps in the funeral industry! Read this carefully.

You should be aware of pay-ahead contracts. If, prior to a death in the family, you contact a funeral home,—you are likely to be offered such a contract.

Selling cemetery lots ahead of time is a long-standing tradition, but the "pre-need (before you need it) funeral market has experienced terrific growth since the late 1980s, especially among the consolidators.

In his 1992 book, *Making End-of-Life Decisions*, Lee Norrgard, consumer affairs analyst for the American Association of Retired Persons (AARP), wrote:

> "Is there adequate consumer protection for buyers of pre-need [funeral and cemetery] plans? At this point, the answer is no. Regulations, investigations, and auditing are minimal in most states. In at least one instance, some of the worst abuses surfaced as a result of private legal actions rather than state enforcement activities . . Buyer beware!"

Medicaid limits as a factor. Medicaid eligibility is one reason why people are willing to pay for their funeral in advance. At the present time, there are no federal limits on the amount that may be set aside for a funeral. But, on the basis that they are administrators of Medicaid, many states do set such limits. The limit in California is $10,000; in Connecticut, $4,800.

There is no limit in New Jersey, so people are really robbed in that state when they sign such pay-ahead contracts. A hidden-camera 20/20 television investigation filmed a funeral director's offer to accept $20,000 for a future funeral, while he assured the potential customer that "any extra" would be returned to the family afterward.

Enormous amounts of money are locked up in prepay funeral and cemetery contracts in America. According to *Consumers Digest,* by the middle of the 1990s, it amounted to over $20 billion. That is probably not an accurate figure, since SCI alone has $3.2 billion in prepayments.

Funeral inflation is running about 5%-7% a year for a full, one-of-everything funeral. Consolidators charge much more. Protection against inflation is a major part of the sales pitch by salesmen, trying to sign you to expensive funeral contracts. But your potential saving will disappear fast if your survivors are pushed into paying additional charges. And this is what usually happens!

Beware of a later billing clause. One item to beware of is this little clause in the contract: "If the death benefits are less than the current retail price at the time of death, an additional amount of funds will be due." *Do not sign an agreement containing that sentence or anything like it!*

In reality, while inflation has increased the cost of living by 2%-3% each year, funeral costs have been increasing by 6%-7% annually. That is why the funeral home or cemetery will want to add that little sentence.

Cash advance items. Another danger is, what is called, the "cash advance" items. These are things which were not mentioned in the written prepay contract—which the funeral home will later charge you for at an inflated price! This includes making out the death certificate, providing the flowers, cemetery expenses, and more besides. One example was the Denver husband which SCI charged $200, just to send four copies of his wife's obituary to area newspapers; yet those newspapers routinely ran them free of charge! These various third-party "cash advance" items, such as flowers, the fee for the organist, or the charge for arranging the obituary, can later be used for a huge increase in the amount of money your survivors will be asked to contribute to your funeral. This is because there was no price cap placed on them in the original contract.

How some people can sleep at night, after going through the day robbing poor widows, is beyond my understanding. But this is going on every day of the year in our land. And it is perfectly legal.

How may the cost of those items be reduced? The survivors should simply tell the funeral home that they, the survivors, will care for those items (flowers, etc.) themselves. But, in practice, many let the funeral home do it—at a great cost to them.

Was the money really put in trust? Another matter to beware of is what part of the money you pay on the contract is actually placed in trust. Let me explain: When you purchase a prepay contract, all the money is supposed to be placed by the funeral home in a bona fide bank trust which cannot be taken by the funeral home and / or cemetery until the funeral and burial occurs.

Prepayment laws in most states require that prepaid funds be placed in trust. But a number of states (California, for example), while requiring

"100% trusting," still provide loopholes. These exceptions may include vaults, burial plots, and memorial stones.

Beware of "constructive delivery." Even in states that require the funeral director to put 100% of your money in trust, there is a way the funeral home can get around that requirement. It is called "constructive delivery." The contract says that the pre-purchased items are stored or warehoused for the customer's future use. But this scheme permits the funeral home or cemetery to not place that money in the trust fund. Then, years later, when you are ready for the funeral and burial, the money may not be there to provide those "constructive delivery" items. Who loses? You do. Yet the thieving firms are rarely punished unless you spend a lot to take them to court.

Few people will demand, in advance, to actually see where their "constructive delivery" items are stored. For that reason, those items rarely are stored. Instead, the firm uses the money for something else—perhaps hoping to repay the money later, if they later have it on hand.

A related problem concerns people who die in a distant state while visiting. The funeral home will refund no money, and transporting the body back home can be costly. These are all factors to be kept in mind.

Another trick: model changes. Another cheat is the method of writing down, on the contract, the name and model number of the casket you selected. But, since models change every six months, later yours may no longer be available when it is needed. So your survivors may be asked for an added fee in order to select a different casket.

The company may be sold. Another problem arises when, between the time you sign the contract and death occurs, the funeral home or cemetery is sold to one of the big consolidators. You can expect that they will figure out ways to later extract more money from the survivors.

Default guarantees may be lacking. As of 1997, only seven states had some sort of guarantee fund to protect consumers against such default. Here are the seven: Florida, Indiana, Iowa, Missouri, Oregon, Vermont, and West Virginia.

Draining the trusts. In 32 states, mortician's associations have set up master trusts. Yet only some of your prepaid funeral money may end up in the trust, dependent on state law. For example, Colorado only requires 75%, permitting the sales agent or funeral director to pocket a 25% commission. Some states permit the funeral home to withdraw an annual "administration fee." Even states requiring 100% trusting permit the undertaker to claim an administrative fee.

Interest charges. Seven states permit interest to be charged by the funeral home on pre-need funeral or cemetery purchases: Florida, Illinois, Indiana, Michigan, Nebraska, North Carolina, and Texas. Virginia specifically forbids such charges.

If you cancel a contract. In addition, you can lose a lot if you try to cancel the agreement ahead of time.

Irrevocable contracts. Another device is the "irrevocable" funeral plan. People do that when they need to shelter assets prior to applying for Social Security or Medicaid.

Morticians love "irrevocable" contracts. Most people think these insure a definitely paid funeral later, when it is needed. But there can be problems. If you later want to change something (for example, from a funeral to a cremation), you may not be able to do so. Yet even an irrevocable contract does not require you to give up all your rights. You may need to contact an attorney if you later want to make changes.

Irrevocable contracts can generally be transferred from one funeral home to another, but few morticians will tell you this.

Eleven questions to ask. If you think you might fund your future death expenses through a trust, here are some questions you should ask before signing anything:

Who is the trustee of the fund? It should not be someone in the funeral home or cemetery association, yet this is permitted in some states.

Who sets up the trust? Is it the funeral home, cemetery, or an outside person?

How much are the trustee fees? They should not be more than .7% to 1.25% maximum. The higher the amount that you place in the trust, the lower should be the percentage of the fee. Larger fees indicate there have been kick-backs to the funeral home, cemetery operator, or someone else.

What investments have already been made by the trust? Ask to see a listing of those investments. If the trust is invested in mutual funds, be aware that those funds might charge their own fee of 2% to 5%, plus another 1% to 2% annually. If the situation does not look good, get out of there fast!

What, in the past, have been the returns on the trust monies invested? They should be quite willing to quickly provide you with this information.

Is the trust truly portable? That is, it should be a plan which you can use, item by item, at any funeral or cemetery facility throughout the nation.

What state agency, if any, oversees the trust fund? Then ask that agency for a report on the trust fund. Doing so will tell you a lot about the fund, and also when it was last audited.

Can the funeral arrangements you make be later changed by family members? If so, what can you now do to prevent that from happening?

Is this an individual trust fund? Unless the law requires it, you do not want this type of trust fund. The fees will probably be higher.

Is it a revocable or irrevocable trust? Can you later cancel it and get your money back?

Is it federally insured? You want this whenever possible.

Should you rely on an insurance policy? An alternative method is to make out an insurance policy, yourself, through an insurance company (instead of letting the funeral director take out the policy for you through the insurance company). Those companies are highly regulated. Their policies are generally more balanced and stable than what your funeral home or cemetery operator can offer you.

But there are still dangers: What are the premiums vs. the face value of the policy? Is the policy guaranteed to cover the cost of the merchandise and services you have selected? Do not accept the policy if it is not guaranteed by the funeral director to cover the costs. What is the growth potential of the policy? What is the rating of the insurance company? What state agency oversees insurance sales in your state? Contact that agency and request information on the company. What commission is being paid? The seller of the policy is required to give you that information. Who is the beneficiary of the funeral policy? It should be the funeral home and not your estate, if you want to avoid taxation. But the funeral home must guarantee that the policy will cover all the funeral expenses you specified.

The underlying problem is that you should not let the funeral director or his business contacts handle your trust. You are safer to work directly through an insurance company yourself, as discussed in the above paragraph. But the best way to set up such a trust is through your local bank. This is called a "totten trust."

Facts about a totten trust. This is the name for a pay-on-death trust account at your local bank. It is not complicated and is the best, safest arrangement for insuring that your money will be used for what you intended, without having been secretly siphoned off by a funeral director. A totten trust will give you the most control and flexibility. It is as safe as the bank it is in. Be sure to name yourself, a close friend, or next of kin—not the mortuary—as the beneficiary of the totten trust. This is a "pay-on-death" account, and it is far safer than entrusting your money to the tender mercies of the funeral industry. In several respects, a totten trust is even safer than an insurance policy.

This is a sort of savings plan that is controlled by you. When you open the account, you deposit a sum of money equal to the cost of the funeral service and wares selected. At any time you can close the account and get your money. These deposits are held as a passbook savings account, certificates of deposit, or money market account, with the earnings helping to defray inflation. An attorney may be needed to set one of these up. Totten trusts are available in every state.

A major benefit of the totten trust is that any excess funds remaining after funeral services is paid to survivors! Also, if you elect to cancel the trust, all principal and interest are returned.

This is not necessarily the case with other popular trusts such as the California Master Trust, Golden Rule, NFDA, and NSM Trusts, which may be paid to the funeral director and an administrative fee retained in the event of cancellation. All funeral home programs generally allow the funeral home to pocket interest on their accounts. So you would be wise to go to a bank and arrange for a totten trust, so you control all the money yourself.

The pre-paid funeral fraud. Before concluding this section, we should mention that some unscrupulous organizations will tell you that a pre-paid funeral is a way to buy-down (lessen) your assets, so you can qualify for state-sponsored (or Medicaid / Medicare) nursing home benefits,—and thus reap a tax-free profit in the process. They will say you can pre-pay an outrageous figure, say $50,000, thereby lowering the patient's net worth to the point his or her nursing home bills will be covered by federal or state programs. Then, when the patient dies, a less expensive funeral arrangement is to be selected with the beneficiary receiving the difference as a tax-free windfall. This is FRAUD, and could result in your imprisonment. Run from any person or establishment making such an offer.

More scams. When someone dies, their name appears in the newspaper. Fraudulent outfits read those notices and prey on the survivors. You may be sent an invoice for something supposedly owed by the deceased. It may be a small bill, but if it has no phone number by which you can verify it, do not pay it.

Another fraudulent activity involves a letter about a supposed insurance policy the deceased had. You will be requested to pay a "processing fee," so they can forward the "death benefits." Legitimate companies do not do this.

Yet another scam will be a letter from a monument company which offers to ship you a grave marker for the deceased. The monument is probably of poor quality, and granite costs about $20.00 per 100 pounds to ship.

ELEVEN WAYS TO CUT COSTS

1 - Pre-arrange the funeral so you will not be

under emotional stress when the death occurs. As explained in the previous chapter, pre-pay for the funeral through a totten trust.

2 - Unless it runs counter to your religious beliefs, you may want to consider a lowest-cost cremation.

3 - Take time, in advance, to select the funeral home you want. Do not wait until a death to do it under hurry and stress. The Federal Trade Commission's Rule requires every funeral home to give you their prices over the phone. While obtaining this information, do not disclose your financial assets. Were your requests sincerely met or were efforts made to steer you in a different direction? Do not sign anything immediately. Take time to think about all you have learned from a variety of sources.

4 - Carefully select the casket you want. Once again, consider all aspects and be slow to make a decision.

5 - Learn whether a vault or grave liner is required by the cemetery, and compare prices for the cheapest one. Check out third-party venders.

6 - Local monument dealers will probably have the lowest-priced ones. Those from funeral dealers and mail order firms are generally more expensive.

7 - Find a local excavation company that will open (dig) and close (cover over) the grave and can satisfy whatever legal and financial roadblocks the cemetery may attempt to place in its way. Outside firms can do it for a much lower price than the cemetery will charge you.

8 - Choose a location for the funeral service that is not in the funeral home. Your church will prob-

ably be the least expensive, and usually there will be no charge.

9 - Consider having a closed-casket visitation among friends and relatives at a private home, not at the funeral home.

10 - Only use one funeral home vehicle, the hearse to transport the deceased. All others will be provided by friends and relatives.

11 - Do not purchase any of the many extras that the funeral home and / or cemetery offers.

All eleven, listed above, involve a funeral home or cremation. Greater savings will accrue from donating the body to a medical school, or conducting a private funeral. For information on both, go to the chapter, *How to Skip the Funeral Industry Entirely*.

PRE-PLANNING THE FUNERAL SERVICE

Planning your own funeral ahead of time will greatly help your survivors when death finally occurs.

On one or more sheets of paper, answer the items listed below. Do this in pencil, in case you later need to change something. Then notify several friends about your sheets, and tell them where you keep it.

1 - Name.

2 - Address.

3 - Phone.

4 - The disposition of my remains should be (funeral, cremation, donation to a medical school, private funeral; state it in as much detail as is needed).

5 - My signature, name printed, date.

6 - First witness to your signature, date.

7 - Second witness, date.

8 - Some information about my life, for an obituary (date and place of birth, previous residences, education, military service, awards, occupation, membership in churches and / or organizations, hobbies, other information, marital status, spouse's name (include maiden name), mother's name, father's name, children, grandchildren, etc.)

9 - What I would like on my tombstone (name, inscription, color and size of stone).

10 - What I would like read to those who attend my funeral.

11 - My religious preference or church membership.

12 - Hymns I would like sung at my funeral.

13 - Pastors I would prefer at my funeral (list several, in order of preference).

14 - If burial, cemetery preference, if any.

15 - If cremation, place of cremation.

16 - List of friends and relatives who should be contacted (names, phone numbers, addresses).

FUNERAL CHECKLIST
STEP-BY-STEP WHAT TO DO

When a loved ones passes away, you suddenly have a lot to do—and hardly know where to start. Here are a few guidelines which will point you in the right direction.

1 - Call a friend to come and be with you.

2 - Get someone to notify friends and family.

3 - Did deceased leave any funeral, etc., directions?

4 - Decide where you want the service to be held (funeral home, church, private home, graveside).

5 - Location of final deposition (cemetery burial, mausoleum, cremation, burial on private land).

6 - If you want a funeral home, select one and call. There are narrow possibilities by requesting price data by phone. Visit, view caskets, get quotes on models. Compare prices by calling Funeral Help Program (FHP): 757-427-0220. They will help you select lower-cost caskets, urns, and vaults. Over the phone, give the model number you selected at the funeral home. Any model can be provided within hours.

7 - Arrange for transfer of remains (if deceased died at a distance from home).

8 - If necessary, get someone to care for deceased's pets and houseplants.

9 - Prepare obituary and send to newspaper.

10 - Viewing period (how many, when, where, cost?).

11 - Accommodations and gathering place for relatives (in someone's home, etc.).

12 - Food preparation (who in charge of, etc.).

13 - Planning the funeral service (when, how long, format, contact minister, which hymns, who rides with whom, and who will need assistance?).

14 - Opening and closing the grave (get prices per day / time).

15 - Is it a military service?

16 - Was there a pre-paid funeral plan or insurance? Does credit plan allow carryover till life in-

surance benefits arrive? Any Veteran's Administration benefits?

17 - Get copies of Statement of Death, Death Certificate. File for Social Security death benefit, file for insurance claim (funeral director may file for all this for you).

18 - After it is all over, leave and go somewhere else and rest for a week.

19 - Decide what to do with pets and house-plants.

20 - Contact attorney, if necessary.

21 - Write thank-you notes and make phone acknowledgments. Beware of phone and letter scams.

22 - Visit monument firms; ask about grade of granite and price of stones. Decide what you want for a marker.

---

5 – HOW TO SKIP THE FUNERAL INDUSTRY ENTIRELY

SEVEN LEVELS OF FUNERAL EXPENSE: CHOOSE THE ONE YOU WANT

Level 1 - You can pay $15,000 to $20,000 for immurement in a mausoleum.

Level 2 - You can pay $3,500 to $8,000 or more for a traditional funeral and in-ground burial.

Level 3 - You can pay $1,500 to $2,000 for a

cremation with memorial service.

Level 4 - You can pay $1,500 to $2,000 for the lowest possible priced direct burial, supervised by a funeral home.

Level 5 - You can pay $400 to $1,500 for a direct cremation, with no extras.

Level 6 - You can pay $30 to $300 for a private funeral (also called a "self-funeral"), which bypasses the funeral industry entirely.

Level 7 - You can pay $0 to $200 for the donation of the body to a medical school (depending on whether they want you to pay to have it shipped to them).

This present chapter deals with Level 6: how to have a private, self-funeral. This is not a funeral of yourself, but a funeral which you, yourself (and possibly some friends), are in charge of—from start to finish.

A FUNERAL WHICH BY-PASSES THE FUNERAL INDUSTRY

In this book, we have surveyed what is happening in the funeral industry. It does appear that there are definite benefits from cremation. The costs are lower and the procedure is far simpler. Yet, there are also disadvantages.

One solution, if you live in a state in which you are legally permitted to do so, is to have what is called a "self-funeral." —This totally sidesteps the funeral industry! It is a way to spend very little on a burial (only a few hundred dollars; most of which may be paid by the Social Security death benefit). Over 40 states in the United States permit this to be done, but the burial must occur fairly rapidly.

The state in which the author lives (Tennessee) permits a person to conduct a complete burial by himself, if he does it within 24 hours after the person dies. There are a number of other states in which this can also be done. You would need to check with your state office. Simply phone your state capital and ask the lady at the main switchboard to connect you with the department which oversees funeral homes and cemeteries.

Lisa Carlson, in her book, *Caring for the Dead: Your Final Act of Love,* provides a state-by-state manual for those living in one of the 42 states where it is legal to by-pass the funeral industry entirely.

Her book discusses self-directed funerals—when you handle the burial of a loved one yourself, without involving an undertaker.

After her husband committed suicide, Carlson decided to not deal with funeral parlors and undertakers because she had almost no money to spare. But, as she explained in her book, there were unexpected healing benefits to handling matters herself. "I felt a strong need to express my love and caring for John, even in death," she wrote.

Description of the procedure. I have a friend who lives nearby who has done some careful research into this matter. Both he and his wife are in their 80s. Recently I interviewed him, and what he told me is a rather complete guide to how to have a non-funeral home funeral. Because the following statement is detailed and very important, we will not place it in smaller print:

"Both I and my wife will be buried in this manner, at almost no expense. We have already helped others. If done within 24 hours, the person can be buried on private property and without going through a funeral home.

"Have someone make you a wooden casket. Ours are lined with cloth, over a half-inch of foam. [Dimensions will be given later in this book.]

"Keep the casket nearby; somewhere in your house, basement, or garage,—where you can get it when you need it.

"The grave must already have been dug; for, at the time of death, it can be difficult to get someone to dig it with a backhoe within 24 hours. If death occurs in the middle of winter (which can easily happen), the ground may be frozen.

"Have someone dig the grave hole on your property or hire a backhoe to do it. State law requires that it be a minimum of four feet deep, so make it a little deeper. If you hit rock, when the burial later takes place, dirt can be piled up a little on top to make up the difference.

"When the grave hole has been dug, place a few boards across the top, with plastic over that to keep out the water. On top of the plastic, put a 4 x 8 piece of plyboard, painted on both sides to keep it from warping (oil base paint will last better than water-based paint).

"We have a private graveyard on our farm. When we dug our graves, we dug a few extra. One never knows when a friend might need it.

"When death is near, bring the casket into the bedroom. When the person dies, you roll him as a person is rolled in a hospital bed in order to change the sheets. In this way, you place a sheet under him. By this time, he has already started to stiffen. So one person lifts him by the head and another by the feet, and both gently place him in the casket. Because only the upper part of the coffin is open (the rest is nailed down), you have to carefully slide him into it.

"As soon as the person dies, immediately apply for a death certificate. Do not call an ambulance! They will carry the body away and you will have problems. Do not let the body leave your place.

"Know in advance the names of the local coroner and assistant coroner. Know their office and home phone numbers and addresses. As soon as the death occurs, immediately go and have the coroner or his assistant sign a death certificate. In order to do this, he will need to know a little about the person who died, cause of death, etc.

"The federal government will give $255 to the family of anyone who dies, to help with burial expense. This is done through Social Security. You need the death certificate in order to claim that money.

"The casket has a lid, plus hooks and eyes, such as are on screen doors to hold the lid shut.

"You have prearranged with someone to deliver a brief message at the burial site. Friends are notified, and the coffin has to be transported to the place of burial. This will require a vehicle which can hold it. You should have determined ahead of time which vehicle, yours or a friend's, will be available for this task.

"At the burial site, friends are gathered and someone, possibly a pastor, gives a little message and quotes some Scripture. Then, as everyone watches, the coffin is lowered into the grave opening.

"At the time the coffin was made, three straps were purchased for use with it. If the person is heavy, three straps are needed, and six men at the funeral lower the casket into the grave. If the person is rather light, only two straps and four men may be needed. These are typical 16-foot tie straps, normally used for tying down things on a truck. Or you can purchase three 16-foot pieces of half-inch nylon cord.

"As the coffin is lowered, everyone is singing. You have either arranged to bring enough shovels for all the men there to use or you have someone with a backhoe present, to cover over the casket.

"All the while, the folk are standing around singing. This brings closure to the event. The activity helps everyone come to full terms with what has happened. It is actually much better than the procedure in a funeral home and gravesite, when the people leave with the grave still open.

"It was a simple service, honoring to God and comforting to all who attended.

"You can afterward erect a marker of some kind at the head of the grave. It can be a tombstone or just a simple wooden marker or cross."

Description of the casket. That concludes the statement. My friend showed me the casket he made for himself. It has a very nice appearance and is built well. He paid a carpenter $250 to make it.

He has another, shorter one for his wife.

His is a straight, rectangular box (instead of the extra-wide at the shoulders and narrow at the foot design of many inexpensive coffins). The shape is like a long house which has a peaked roof, with a 22° pitch. The wood is three-quarter-inch stock, and is not plyboard. It looks like a good grade of pine. My friend covered the exposed wood with linseed oil, giving it a varnished appearance. While it looks elegant, yet it cost very little. The fact that the box has not been painted will help it return to the earth more quickly, in accordance with the statement in Genesis 3:19.

Looking at it from one end, here are the dimensions: It is shaped like a peaked-roof house. The bottom is 25½" across, 10¾" high; and each of the peaked sides of the roof are 15". The center measure from base to the top of the peak is 17½".

Looking at it from the side, the box is 75½" long (my friend is 71" tall). But the length would change in accordance with the height of the person.

Looking at it from the top, the two slanted sides of the roof (as are all other parts of the box) are nailed solid with countersunk finishing nails. But, at the head end, both slanted top sides are hinged 25½" back from the front. They fold back over the top. When closed, the front edges extend out over the front of the casket 2½". That was done so two hooks on the front of the box can fasten into two eyes which are screwed into this overhang. This provides a way to fasten ("seal") the casket shut.

There are two hinges on each peaked top side

of the "roof" of the casket. Each of the four hinges are set 2" from opposing edges of the roof boards. This is why, when the two halves of the lid are opened, they lay straight back over the roof.

The entire roof is nailed to four triangular boards: the two end boards of the casket and two triangular pieces, spaced apart, located below the rear and nailed-down part of the roof. Each triangular board is 5-5/8" high by 24" wide at its outer base points.

Looking inside the box is done by opening the hinged top and laying them back. Inside, the casket is lined (bottom and sides) with ½" foam, overlaid with white sheeting. (The outside width of the casket is 25½", and the inside width—from one inner edge of the inside lining to the other—is 22".) A small 11" x 3" pillow is at the head, made with the same quality sheeting over 3" foam. It all has a high-quality appearance, yet at a very economical cost. Surely, our Lord and Saviour would approve of such a combination of economy and nice taste.

The making of the casket could be decidedly simplified by giving it a flat top instead of one that is peaked. If that was done, the outside dimensions of the ends and the sides would be about 17 inches.

An additional factor should be taken into account: There is only 8¼ inches from the top, center of the cushion (and 9¼ inches from pressed-down cushion) to the triangular cross-piece supporting the peaked roof. This might provide enough space for a person with a large front-to-back girth. An extra inch or two in height should be added for some people.

Private burial. Local zoning regulations might be a factor in urban areas. But if you live in a rural location, you should encounter no problems if you bury a loved one on private land.

The burial sites must be some distance from any water supply. The slope of the land and the soil conditions must also be taken into consideration, especially where the earth is shallow, or above a rock or clay. Power lines should be avoided (because overhead power may later be replaced by a buried cable).

If you establish a family burial plot on your property, and it goes into the deed, this can be a problem in the later sale of the land. A graveyard becomes a permanent easement on the property in many states. In a 1959 case in Oklahoma (*Heiligman vs. Chambers*), a grandson sued to keep the new landowner from moving family bodies to a town cemetery. The court decision upheld the right to permanency of a family burial plot. But some other states have provisions for moving the graves from "abandoned" burial sites.

Unless a family burial plot is registered in the county clerk's office in the courthouse, the plot will not be recognized as a family burial plot.

If you want to explore this possibility. Is there a way you can avoid paying a funeral director when a loved one dies? A growing number of people are doing just that. Unfortunately, there is not a lot of information available on the subject. But one outstanding book is available! It is Lisa Carlson's *Caring for the Dead: Your Final Act of Love*. You will find it listed at the back of this present book, under the section, *"Where to Obtain Further Infor-*

mation.

Here are a few suggestions: First, check into the funeral home situation in advance! This is extremely important. If you might decide to have a funeral home director care for the death of a loved one—and you may decide it is best to do just that,—then phone around in advance and get prices. You need information; and, if at all possible, you want to obtain it earlier rather than later.

Whether or not you want to care for a funeral yourself (a "self-funeral"), learn what the state laws are by phoning the state capital and asking them to send you information. Learn what you can and cannot do. If you can build a casket yourself, arrange for a local carpenter to construct one. It can be a simple pine box. Your deceased loved one will no longer exist until the resurrection, and the type of box he is buried in will not really change the situation in the slightest degree. It is God that your faith must be in, not the durability of the coffin. Actually, to fulfill Genesis 3:19, you want a casket which will eventually crumble.

Check on requirements for transporting the body, whether the casket can be buried anywhere (including on your own property) or only in a graveyard. Check on graveyard prices and requirements.

Actually, at the time a loved one dies, there is an advantage in knowing things you need to do. It helps you through this difficult time. In addition, you are doing another last thing for your loved one. That is comforting also.

One individual who buried her father said, "Handling my father's burial myself helped me become more involved. There was no intermediary trying to explain to me the benefits of satin lining for motives that I'm sure had to do with something other than my own best interest and my father's best interest."

For many people, the time when a loved one passes away is a time when funds are especially low and almost absent. If you can, plan in advance and save the greater part of funeral expenses. This is what the one who will be buried or cremated would want.

Funerals should not put you in debt. We do not need that, and our beloved dead would not want that for us either.

Here is additional information you should know, if you wish to handle a funeral yourself.

If the death occurs in a hospital. Some hospitals may be hesitant to release the body to you. If the death was expected, it is well to notify them ahead of time of your intentions. If they are still uncertain, a phone call from your attorney will clarify matters to them. It is crucial that you immediately obtain that death certificate. Many hospitals do not have facilities for storage of a dead person, and want it immediately transported to a funeral home.

If organs are to be donated, this should be immediately cared for before the body leaves the hospital. See *"Medical Gifts"* for more on this.

If there is a delay in moving the body (especially if it has to be moved from one state to another), embalming may be necessary (although most air carriers will waive that requirement if there are religious objections). Refrigeration or dry ice can substitute.

If the body must be transported. Never move a body without a permit or medical permission. Always call ahead, even if you have a permit.

If you are transporting the body for cremation, place it in a simple covered box. It cannot be over 38 inches wide or 30 inches high, because that is the standard size of the cremation chamber. Do not exceed those dimensions. A container that is 24 inches wide by 14 to 18 inches high is usually sufficient. The length of the box will determine the type of vehicle transporting it.

Simple cardboard containers can be purchased from most funeral homes. If you know in advance that death is imminent, for a list of good, low-cost sources you can contact:

funerals/org/famsa/caskets.htm

A permit for transportation or final deposition is required by most states. First complete the death certificate (we earlier discussed how to do that even on weekends). A special permit-to-cremate is needed prior to cremation. If death occurs at night or on a weekend, contact a local funeral director for that permit. As a deputy for the state in this matter, he should not charge for this unless such a charge is specified by state law.

All states honor the transportation permits of another state. But final disposition is governed by the state the remains are going to. Check by phone before starting the trip. You may need a burial permit, if final deposition will be in a cemetery or on private land.

Several companies specialize in shipping bodies. Inman Nationwide is one of them. It has contracted with local funeral homes to serve as agents in every state. It pays those agents $575 for, what is called, "forwarding remains." An additional mileage change may be added if far from the nearest airport. Airfare is extra, of course. (Keep in mind that, even if you want a funeral home to care for the funeral at the destination, if the funeral home on the receiving end wants to charge you more than $575, you will save money by working directly with a shipping company, such as Inman.)

Special problems. Fluids may leak from body orifices, so absorbent towels or newspapers can be placed under the deceased. Place him in a sheet.

If he died of a communicable disease, take health precautions (such as a pair of latex rubber gloves). The state may require participation by a funeral director in such a situation.

If an autopsy has been performed or death has occurred from injury, the body can be wrapped in a vinyl body bag (obtainable from a funeral director), to prevent additional leakage. A plastic, zippered mattress cover can be substituted. Avoid plastic, if possible, if the remains are to be cremated.

Your own private cemetery. As mentioned above, you may need a burial permit, if it will be in a cemetery or on private land. The top of the coffin should be at least three feet below the natural surface of the earth. The burial location should be 150 feet from a water supply and outside the right-of-way easement of any utility or power lines.

Private cemeteries, also known as family cemeteries, were as common as church cemeteries until well into the 20th century, especially in rural areas. It was common for families to bury their deceased on a hillside or somewhere behind the house on the property they owned.

Non-funeral home cremation. If a cremation, which sidesteps the funeral home, is intended, a cremation permit is often needed from the local coroner or medical examiner. The deceased may have signed such a form; if he did not, authorization from next of kin is required by most crematories.

If the person died in a distant place or next of kin live far away, a fax, Western Union, or overnight mail can quickly bring the required authorization for cremation.

Location of crematories. If you want to bypass the funeral home and have cremation done, you need to work directly with a crematory. There are nearly 1,200 of them in the U.S. and about 140 in Canada. Check your state funeral board or the Yellow Pages, to locate the one nearest you.

Some crematories expect to be paid at the time a body is delivered, even if insurance or other death benefits are expected. Others will bill you.

Pacemakers in a cremation. If the deceased had a pacemaker, you will need to remove it. It is about the size of a silver dollar and is embedded just under the skin, generally near the neck or lower on the rib cage. A shallow cut will easily remove it. If not taken out, the pacemaker may explode in the chamber, seriously damaging the chamber. That is not a bill you want to pay!

The legal next of kin. Who is the legal "next of kin"? They are generally determined in this order: (1) the surviving spouse, (2) all adult sons and daughters, (3) parents, (4) all adult siblings, or (5) guardian or "person in charge." If permission can be obtained from the first on the list, the permission of those further down on the list are not needed. Keep in mind that a crematory will hesitate to cremate if it knows the relatives are arguing about the matter. Courts will generally defer to the wishes of the deceased, if it is known.

The obituary notice. If you are managing the death privately, you will need to arrange for an obituary in your local newspaper. Phone the paper and learn its policies and any costs before writing the obituary. They may want a standard format or expect certain information. Try to mention any services planned, including a later memorial service that might be held. You can phone or fax in the obituary notice (it is called an "obit"). Because no funeral director is involved, the paper may want to see (or have you fax in a copy of) the death certificate. The newspaper may or may not charge anything. Big-city papers generally only list prominent individuals. Frankly, the newspaper is likely to charge less or nothing if a funeral home is not handling the case.

When a private funeral is not difficult. You have learned a lot of facts which could prove invaluable if you would wish to conduct a truly "private" (non-funeral industry) funeral and burial. But did you notice that certain things can make a "self-funeral" more difficult? Here are important things to consider:

    1 - It is easiest if the person dies at home.

    2 - It can be somewhat more difficult if he dies in a hospital. This is due to the fact that state laws must be explained to the staff, so you can take the deceased instead of having the body sent to a funeral home. Therefore, you want to explain the situation early on, preparing them for what is ahead.

    3 - It would be significantly more difficult if the person dies at a location distant from his home. The transportation costs might be such, that a local cremation or funeral in that area may considered as an option.

    4 - It is easiest if the person can be buried quickly.

    5 - The situation becomes more difficult if lots of relatives want to arrive days later and want to view the body. (The solution is a memorial visitation, without the casket being present. In reality, the deceased was probably quickly buried.)

    Three that are lowest in cost. From data here and later in this book, you will discover that the three lowest-cost ways to care for your deceased are:

    1 - Donate the body to a medical school (if they accept it; three will definitely accept it). You can include a proviso to return the cremated remains later. (They probably cover all costs, but sometimes they want you to pay transportation costs if it is rejected.)

    2 - Conduct a home funeral, by-passing the funeral industry. (The cost is primarily the homemade casket, about $250.)

    3 - Contact your nearest crematory yourself, and have a direct cremation. This also by-passes the funeral home. (The cost may vary from $250 to

$1000.)

PREPARING
THE DEATH CERTIFICATE
YOURSELF

Some people consider the death certificate to be an especially difficult hurdle. But once you are acquainted with it, you will find it to be something you can handle,—as long as you write carefully, completely, and provide accurate information.

All American death certificates are based on the U.S. Standard Certificate of Death, although slight variations may exist in some states. At the present time, the 1978 revision of the certificate is in effect.

The form is not complicated, but it must be completed carefully. Any error or omission, even in the portion that is filled out by a physician, can delay your plans for disposition of the body or subject family members to questioning at a later time.

It is very important that you type all entries or print very legibly in black ink. Complete each item; and, unless otherwise stated below, leave no blanks. Make no alterations or erasures, avoid abbreviations, verify spelling of names, and have original signatures (no rubber stamps). Fill it out slowly and thoughtfully, so you will make no mistakes.

(In order to simplify the process, make a photocopy of the death certificate, and fill it out in pencil. When fully satisfied that everything is correct, make a second copy, carefully typed or printed in ink with signatures.)

Here are key points:

"1. Decedent—Name: First, Middle, Last." Give full names, no initials.

"2. Sex." Write "male" or "female." Do not leave blank.

"3. Date of Death (Month, Day, Year)." Write out the month, do not use numbers. If a person died exactly at midnight, he is considered to have died on the day just ended, not the next day.

"4. Race." For groups other than "White, Black, American Indian," give the national origin (Chinese, Korean, etc.)

"5. Age." There are three lines; only fill out one (a. over a year old; b. infants under a year; c. infant death within the first day.)

"6. Date of Birth (Month, Day, Year)." Use the full or abbreviated name of the month, not a number.

"7. Place of Death." Give county, city, or town where death occurred. Give hospital, institution, or address of home where occurred. *Line 7b* is filled out if he was a patient at a hospital or dead on arrival there. If death occurred in a vehicle, etc., list place of address where body was first removed from conveyance. If death occurred in the air or outside the U.S., contact the state office of vital statistics for instructions.

"8. State of Birth." If you do not know it, write: "U.S.—Unknown." Do not leave this space blank!

"9. Citizen of what country." If born or naturalized as U.S. citizen, write "U.S.A." Otherwise list country where held citizenship.

"10. Married," etc. Enter marital status at time of death. A person is legally married, even though separated. If not known, write "Unknown." Do not leave blank.

"11. Surviving Spouse (if wife, include maiden name)." If married, this information is needed for insurance and other survivor benefits. If not married, write "Not married."

"12. Was Decedent Ever in U.S. Armed Forces?" Write "Yes," "No," or "Unknown." Do not leave blank.

"13. Social Security Number." Do not leave blank.

"14. Occupation and Industry of Decedent." Give this information if 14 years or older, even if he was retired, disabled, or institutionalized when died. Line **14a** asks for "usual occupation." Give the kind he did most of his life, not last job held. Do not write "retired." "Student" is acceptable if he was a young person who died while a student and was never regularly employed. **Line 14b** asks for the kind of business or industry to which his usual occupation was related (farming, hardware store, government, etc.). Do not write a firm or organization name.

"15. Residence of Decedent." Where he actually resided, not where he died. Never enter a temporary address during a visit, vacation, etc. But place of residence while on military duty or in college is not considered temporary, and should be entered as the residence. Nursing homes, prisons, etc., would also be included as place of residence. If a child, residence is the same as for the parents or legal guardian (unless the child was living in an institution where individuals usually stay for a long period of time).

Under residence address, if there is no street name, write the rural route or post office box number and whether he resided within the municipal boundaries of the city or town.

"16-17. Parentage." Enter full names (first, middle, last) of his father and mother. Give mother's maiden name.

"18. Identity of Informant." Name and full mailing address of person who furnished the personal facts. If it is you, enter your own name and address.

"19. Type and Place of Disposition." Write whether it will be burial, cremation, entombment, etc. If a gift for medical science, write "Removal— Donation," and specify the name and location of the institution in later lines. **Line 19b** asks for the name of the cemetery, crematory, or institution where deceased was placed. **Line 19c** asks for the location.

"20. Funeral Service Licensee Information." **Line 20a** is signed by "funeral service licensee or person acting as such." If no funeral director is involved and you are completing the death certificate, your signature should be written here. **Line 20b** asks for "name of the facility." If no funeral director is involved, you avoid confusion by entering your relationship to the deceased or, if you are working with a church group, the name of the church group. *Line 20c* asks for "address of facility." You may list your home address or address of the church group.

"21. Certification: Physician." *Note: Read below under Line 22, before filling out Line 21.* The attending physician or family doctor should fill this out. If certification is required by the medical examiner or coroner, this space should be left blank. As the "person acting as funeral direct," your only role is to make sure the lines are filled in correctly, to avoid later inconvenience for you or family members. *Line 21a* asks for the signature of the doctor who certifies the death. *Line 21b* asks the date the certificate was signed. *Line 21c* asks the exact time of death. Give it in hours and minutes, local time. *Line 21d* asks the "name of attending physician if other than certifier." If the certifier is the attending physician, that space should be left blank.

"22. Certification: Medical Examiner or Coroner." *This should be filled out instead of Line 21 if a medical examiner or coroner is involved.* Lines *22a* through *22c* are identical to counterparts in Line 21.

"23. Name and Address of Certifier." Write the name and address of the person whose signature appears in Items 21a or 22a.

"24. Registrar—Signature and Date Received." The local official (registrar) will sign and date the form here at the time it is filed. This "regis-

trar" may be the county clerk in the courthouse.

"25. Cause of Death." The physician, coroner, or medical examiner whose signature appeared on lines 21a or 22a will fill out this line. It is extremely important that the section be filled out properly, so the "person acting as funeral director" should review it to be sure there are no hasty errors. This section is divided into two parts:

"Part 1." Enter only one cause of death on each line in Part 1. Do not list the general mode of dying (such as heart failure, respiratory failure). They want something more specific than a final problem.

Line a asks for the immediate cause of death. This is the disease, injury, or complication that directly preceded death. It can be the sole entry, if only one condition was present at death. There must be an entry on line a. In case of a violent death, write the actual cause (crushed chest, fractured skull, etc.). If a specific cancer or injury, give the site (pancreas, left lung, etc.)

Line b asks what disease, injury, or complication, if immediate cause of any, gave rise to the direct or immediate cause of death reported above. In other words, what condition prepared the way for the immediate cause of death (even if a long interval of time has elapsed since the onset of that condition). If an injury, the form of external violence or accident which led to the killing injury (auto accident, struck by falling tree, etc.)

Line c asks what condition, *if any*, gave rise to the antecedent condition on line b. If the deceased had more than three casually related conditions leading to death, add lines d, e, etc.

The final line should state the condition which the physician feels is the underlying cause of death; that is, the condition that started the sequence of events between normal health and the immediate cause of death.

Because health departments often complain that this section is not filled out properly by the medical person, you may be able to help provide the needed medical history.

There is *space* provided at the end of lines a, b, and c for recording the interval between the onset and death for the immediate cause, antecedent condition, if any, and underlying cause. These time intervals usually are established by the physician on the basis of the available information. The time of onset may not be known, in which case the physician can write "Unknown." Do not leave this space blank.

"Part 2." The physician should write on this line any other important disease or condition that was present at the time of death that may have contributed to death, but was not related to the immediate cause of death.

"26. Autopsy." Write "Yes" if a partial or complete autopsy was performed. Otherwise, enter "No." Do not leave this blank.

"27. Was Case Referred to Medical Examiner or Coroner?" When the cause of death is certified by an attending physician, this line is to be completed. Write "Yes" if the Medical examiner or coroner was contacted regarding this case. Otherwise, "No."

"28. Accident or Injury." Fill out this section only if death resulted from an accident or injury. Such deaths are usually certified by a medical examiner or coroner, who will complete this section. Otherwise, it should be completed by the attending physician. *Line 28a*: Specify whether death was caused by accident, suicide, homicide, undetermined, or is pending investigation. *Lines 28b-28c*: Enter year, month, day, and exact time of injury. *Line 28d*: Briefly state how the injury occurred ("fell off ladder while painting house," etc.) *Line 28e* asks whether injury occurred at work. Enter "Yes," "No," or "Unknown." In *line 28f*, enter the type of place where the injury occurred (home, farm, street, office building, etc.) In *line 28g*, enter complete address of the location of the injury.

"29. Origin or Descent." This is a question asked in some, but not all states. One format asks "Was the decedent of Spanish origin?" Specify "Yes" or "No." If "Yes," specify Mexican, Cuban, etc.

The second format says "Origin or descent." List the nationality of the deceased or his ancestors, prior to coming to America (Italian, Mexican, English, etc.). The exception to this would be American Indians and Alaskan natives. Those migrating ancestors might be quite distant in the past. Do not list percentages (part Italian, part Irish, etc.). It should be what the deceased thought he was. If he did not identify with any foreign nationality, write "American." Do not list a religious group here. Note that the answer here might be the same or different than was given in question 4.

ORGANIZING
A CHURCH FUNERAL COMMITTEE

Before concluding this section on self-help funerals, it should be mentioned that you might wish to organize a funeral committee in your area. It might be among members of your church. You would need to explain to friends what is involved and decide on what your group will do. The result, of course, would be near-free funerals for those your group wishes to help. Think of how many poor widows you could help! Some time would be involved, but not very much outlay of money. What you would be providing would be help in arranging the self-funeral or direct cremation.

Nine ways to help others. Here are the nine possible areas of help this would involve. You can quickly see that each death would involve only a brief, limited amount of work; yet it is such practical benefit!

1 - Obtaining the death certificate and other needed permits. Someone in the group would need to be familiar with those papers and information required for them, state regulations, and local officials. They would need to know who to contact during off-hours. Someone would have to be available to help with this, even in the middle of the night.

2 - Have some pine boxes already prepared. Extra standard, long boxes could be kept on hand. Each one might cost a couple hundred dollars to make, but the survivors could pay for it from death benefits. Expect to occasionally not be repaid for a box. Have some small sizes on hand for infants and small children. In order to locate individuals who could make them for you, on the web go to:

funerals.org/famsa/caskets.htm

3 - A vehicle(s) to transport the body. A van, pickup, or station wagon would be needed. Two or more people to help lift the load. Unusual transportation situations might arise, so it is well to be prepared.

4 - Bathing the body and putting on clothes could be done, but would not be necessary if the deceased must be buried within 24 hours. It would also not be necessary if an immediate cremation were to take place. But shrouds should be available. If nothing else is available, these can consist of new, white bed sheets.

5 - Shelter for the body. In those instances in which immediate burial or cremation will not occur (due to inclement weather or relatives arriving from a distance, etc.), a secluded, cool place will be needed to store the body. This could be in a home or in a backroom of the church. In summer months, especially, that room should be air conditioned.

6 - The immediate needs of the family would need to be provided for. This could include providing meals, housecleaning, baby-sitting, shopping, answering the phone, and especially having someone they could talk to. Pets might need to be cared for. If the deceased lived alone, care for incoming mail, and pay utilities.

7 - Notify relatives and others close to the family. Employers will need to be contacted. As requested, write to others. Pick up arriving out-of-town guests and relatives. Provide lodging and local transportation for them.

8 - Set up a registry. It should list (1) relatives to be contacted for church members, especially those living alone; (2) final disposition preferences (body and / or organ donation, body burial, cremation); (3) disposition of cremated remains or body burial location. The memorial societies have a form for one to fill out, to help organize this data. Called *"Putting My House in Order,"* it can be obtained from your regional memorial society or from funerals.org.

9 - Contact key people, in advance, and let them know what you are doing—especially if you will not be working through a local funeral home. This would include: local town clerk (and / or local coroner or medical examiner), hospitals, nursing homes, and anyone else who might be involved. (It is helpful to have a copy of the state funeral regulations, so you can refer to it if necessary.) Do not be antagonistic if you meet people who are not clear about the legality of this. Gently inform them. Their concern is merely to be responsible in their own jobs.

In most states, by law, your congregation or group can work with the family and provide all the arrangements when a member dies. But you might wish to work through a local funeral home. Of course, if you take that route, costs will spiral somewhat! A basic factor is the reliability of your group of volunteers to be there to help when a death occurs. One thing for sure: This is practical Christianity in action, and it will be deeply appreciated.

FACTS ABOUT ORGAN DONATIONS AND MEDICAL GIFTS

Body donation. It should briefly be mentioned that there is yet another way to avoid a funeral. This is the donation of the body for medical research. It will primarily be used as a cadaver for medical students to dissect, as part of their medical training.

Such a donation, of course, would totally eliminate the funeral and all its expenses. You would receive nothing for the donation and would pay nothing. This is the very simplest way to avoid the funeral industry.

The August 1961 issue of the *Reader's Digest* had an article, *"Let the Dead Teach the Living,"* which explained the critical shortage of cadavers for anatomical study in medical schools. The article said this: "Every individual who bequeaths his remains to a medical school makes an important contribution to the advance of human knowledge."

Frightened at such a prospect, the *National Funeral Service Journal* made this comment:

"This is a practice that cannot openly be opposed without branding the funeral directors as being indifferent to the health and welfare of mankind . . The loss of a casket sale will create a financial blow in those cases where the body is contributed to a medical school. Fortunately, such cases are infrequent at the present time; unfortunately, they may become more frequent in the future."

Organ transplants. Organ transplants are becoming increasingly successful, so you should consider whether you wish your body to be used for medical use ("body donation") or for organ transplants.

The corneas of elderly persons can usually be used, and eyes may be donated even if total body donation to a medical school is subsequently planned. Skin can also be used.

The donation of eyes and other organs must be done under sterile conditions and usually within a short time after death. If such donations are desired, the next of kin should make this decision known to attending hospital staff at the earliest possible time.

The uniform donor card. You can specify, on your donor card, which has priority: organ donation or body donation. For example, you can specify that, only if your organs are not needed, is your body to be considered for body donation. You can also write on the card that your body can be considered for body donations only if your organs are not needed (because of mutilation during an auto accident or major thoracic incision during a failed operation, etc.), that you want to be buried in a plain pine box. Because you donated your body, they are required to bury it free of charge if it is not acceptable for donation.

Many medical schools request that a *Uniform Donor Card* be filled out as part of the process of making a bequest. Such cards can also be obtained from many other sources, including kidney foundations, eye banks, and funeral planning societies.

The *Uniform Donor Card* includes information that is consistent with the *Anatomical Gifts Acts*, legislation which has been adopted by nearly all states.

Here is the information on the front side of a sample donor card:

UNIFORM DONOR CARD

Of _____

In the hope I may be able to help others, I make this anatomical gift, if medically acceptable, to take effect upon my death. The words and marks below indicate my desires.

I give: (a) ___ any needed organ or parts.
        (b) ___ only the following organs or parts.

_____

(specify the organs or parts)

for transplantation, therapy, medical research or education;

        (c) ___ my body for anatomical study if needed.

Limitations or special wishes if any _____

_____

This is the back side of a sample donor card:

Signed by the donor and the following two witnesses in the presence of each other:

_____   _____

    Signature of Donor   Date of Birth

_____   _____

    Date Signed   City and State

_____

           Witness

_____
Witness

If you check *Line A* ("any needed organs"), it means that they will take precedence over the possibility of your entire body being used. It may still be used, but the donated organs will come first. Donation of a major organ (such as the kidneys being removed for a kidney transplant) will render it unlikely that a medical school would want the body.

If you check *Line B* ("only the following organs or parts"), you will write in only certain organs which can be used for transplants.

By checking *Line C*, you have specified that your entire body can, if acceptable, be used.

Your signature must be witnessed by two other people who also sign the card.

Some individuals specify only one medical school; most do not care which ones may use their body.

In most states, you can also specify on your driver's license your willingness to donate your organs. But you are also expected to carry a Uniform Donor's Card with you.

Other facts about the giving of organs. Here is an address to contact if you wish to donate organs: The Living Bank, P.O. Box 6725, Houston, TX 77265. Phone: 713-528-2971. You can also contact any local hospital. Virtually any hospital can either service this request and supply the required forms or refer you to an organ bank that can.

The transfer of the organs is done entirely anonymously. Neither party knows the other.

There are thousands of people waiting for the donation of various organs, especially corneas and kidneys.

Although funeral directors are trained for the removal of corneas, the specified organs must be removed shortly after death and in a sterile environment. Generally, this can only be done effectively if the person has died in a hospital. But next of kin should be notified by the donor in advance. It should also be placed on the hospital chart.

When a person unexpectedly dies in an auto accident, etc., hospital staff may suggest to next of kin that an organ donation may, if desired, be made.

If the death occurs in a home, and the family will be handling all funeral arrangements (without the help of a funeral home), the area Eye Bank can send a technician to remove the corneas. Please understand that this does not in any way disfigure the body, and does not preclude an open casket viewing later.

No one will be paid for the organs donated, and most medical organizations involved will pay all costs for transport of organs and / or body. If you specify that only a certain medical school can have your body, and that school does not pay transportation costs, your next of kin would have to pay it! That might be a matter to check on ahead of time.

It is well for the donor's family to hold only a memorial service (without the body being present). In this way, the body can be transported as soon as possible. Of course, if a body is donated, the next of kin, or a friend, would have the responsibility of sending the obituary to the newspaper.

Later cremation. Since most bodies are used within a two-year period, many medical schools cremate the remains when the study is finished and bury it in a dedicated plot. —But if (if) the school is notified at the time of body donation or delivery, those remains can, at the time of cremation, be returned to the family. However, since this option is not available at all medical schools, you might wish to specify on the donor card that the body only go to a school which will later return the cremains to the relatives. The school should be notified if a change of address occurs during that two-year period.

The possibility of rejection. If the body is rejected, the next of kin will have the responsibility of selecting an alternative, such as a funeral or cremation. But there are three medical institutions which, if you contract with them for the donation, will definitely accept the body, regardless of its condition: The University of South Alabama, the State Anatomy Board of Maryland, and Southwestern Medical School in Texas. Please understand that they do not promise to use the body. They might just cremate and bury the cremains. All other schools reserve the right to refuse a donation.

Why would a school refuse a body? If they already have too many donations, if the body is in a deteriorated condition, if it is mutilated, or has limbs or major organs missing. They may refuse the very elderly (over 80), very young (a child or infant), severe burn victim, surgery at or near time of death, over 6 feet tall, obesity, or having a contagious disease, such as tuberculosis, AIDS, meningitis, systemic cancer, Alzheimer's, Creutzfeld-Jacob (mad cow disease), etc.

GOVERNMENT BENEFITS FOR DECEASED U.S. VETERANS

If the deceased is a United States veteran, he or she can request and receive a free burial. Here is additional information and contacts:

When contacting the government, the following information will be needed:

Full name and military grade.

Uniformed Service (Branch).

Social Security Number.

VA claim number (if assigned and known).

Date and place of birth.

Date of retirement or honorable separation from active duty.

Date and place of death.

Copy of separation papers, such as DD Form 214.

Here are addresses you may need:

• U.S. veterans are entitled to burial in a national cemetery. For information, contact Superintendent, Arlington National Cemetery, Arlington, VA 22211-5003. Phone: 703-695-3250 or 703-695-3255.

• U.S. veterans are entitled to burial at sea. Contact Retired Activities Section (Pers-662c), Bureau of Naval Personnel, Washington D.C. 20370-6620. Phone: 800-255-8950 / 703-614-3197.

• VA flag (for veteran's casket, presentation to family). Available from VA by filling out VA Form 2008. Also available from many post offices. Phone: 800-827-1000.

• Presidential memorial certificates (PMC) program. Apply at nearest VA regional office.

• VA transportation and burial allowance. Contact nearest VA regional office, to inquire about eligibility. A number of limitations have been placed on these allowances in recent years, but anyone receiving (or qualified to receive) disability should investigate. Allowances run $150, $300, or $1,500.

• VA headstones and markers. Contact Office of Memorial Programs (403), Department of Veteran Affairs, 810 Vermont Avenue NW, Washington, D.C. 20420. Phone: 800-827-1000. Ask for Form 40-1330. (Some funeral directors have this form available.)

• Military honors. Virtually anyone who served on active duty in the military can receive graveside honors including a rifle salute, the playing of *Taps* by a bugler, and the flag ceremony. Phone the nearest military base (including ROTC and recruiting stations) or a veterans organization. The American Legion, Veterans of Foreign Wars (VFW), and American Veterans (AMVETS) can either provide you with these services or direct you to where to obtain them.

• Donating the body of a military person to science. Contact Uniformed Services University of Health Sciences, 4301 Jones Bridge Road, Bethesda, MD 20814-4799. Phone: 301-295-3333.

6 – MORE FACTS WORTH KNOWING

HOW THE MEMORIAL SOCIETIES CAN HELP YOU

For a number of readers, this will be the most important part of this book. There are actually non-profit groups who want to help you have a simple, low-cost funeral!

The memorial societies (also called funeral societies and memorial associations) are composed of people who have banded together to help people have inexpensive alternatives to a "standard funeral." The societies provide guidance on obtaining a simple, low-cost funeral and burial. As you might expect, the funeral industry is terrified of them.

The "concepts of the memorial society" are stated in one of their earlier pamphlets, *Memorial Associations: What They Are, How They Are Organized,* published by the *Cooperative League of the USA.*

"Memorial associations and their members seek modesty, simplicity, and dignity in the final arrangements over which they have control. This concern for spiritual over material values has revealed that a 'decent burial' or other arrangement need not be elaborate . .

"Some families wish to avoid funerals and burials altogether. The prefer cremation and a memorial service later . . without an open casket and too many flowers.

"Still others want to will their bodies to a medical school for teaching and research. They also may offer their eyes to an eye bank so the corneas may be transplanted and the blind may see.

"Whether it's an unostentatious funeral, a simple burial, cremation, a memorial service, or a concern for medical science, these people want dignified and economical final arrangements. Accordingly they have organized several kinds of memorial associations in more than a dozen states and several Canadian provinces."

These societies are now in nearly every state in America. *You will find a rather complete list of them at the back of this book.*

Some of the societies function as educational organizations and limit themselves to advocacy of 'rationally pre-planned final arrangements.' Most, have gone further and, through collective bargaining, have secured contracts with one or more funeral establishments, to supply the 'simple funeral' for members at an agreed-on sum.

Some societies emphasize cremation, others are more interested in donating bodies to medical schools, while still others focus on freedom of choice in the matter of burials.

All of them are nonprofit—truly nonprofit—organizations, open to anybody to join. Each is run by unpaid boards of directors. Enrollment fees are very low, generally about $20 for a "life membership." But a few groups collect annual fees. The money is used for printings, mailings, and administrative expenses. Because most of them do no advertising, many people are unaware of their existence. Over the years, the press has said very little about them.

A primary objective is to make it easier for people to hold memorial services and receive inexpensive funerals—without having to argue with morticians over prices, features, add-ons, and unexpected charges. They tend to hold in disfavor those things which bring regular funeral homes and cemeteries the most money: embalming and open viewings in needlessly expensive caskets, an abundance of expensive flowers, expensive mausoleum crypts, or high-priced cremation urns in columbarium niches.

Actually, a memorial service by a society will be exactly what the survivors want it to be. It may be a private gathering in a home or a large church service. The only distinguishing feature is the absence of the corpse and the casket. The loved one is quickly buried (or cremated) and a memorial service is then held. All very simple and inexpensive.

For additional information, contact the memorial society in your area. If you do not know how to locate it, turn to the list at the back of this book. If you are still unable to make contact, phone their clearinghouse, Funeral Consumers Alliance (FCA) office at 800-765-0107. Founded in 1968, the FCA has helped many people. Its address is FCA, P.O. Box 10, Hinesburg, VT 05461.

SIGNIFICANT STATE STATUTES

Each state has its own set of regulations governing funerals and the burying of the dead. Some have been mentioned in this book.

For a much more complete list, you will want to contact the *Funeral Consumers Alliance* (FCA) office at 800-765-0107. Their website, funerals.org, will also provide some information.

Part Two (pp. 177-605) of Lisa Carlson's book, *Caring for the Dead,* will provide you with an overview of regulations in all 50 states. Her book is published by FCA, which is the central clearing house for the memorial societies. You may want to contact the nearest one to you.

Here are a few key regulations. Please be aware of the fact that regulations can, and do, change from time to time!

Which states have special regulations? Which states permit you to keep the cremains (ashes) from a cremation? *All states.*

Which states prohibit the private scattering of ashes? *Only California.*

Which states restrict casket sales to funeral homes, thus forbidding other firms to compete with them? *Alabama, Georgia, Idaho, Louisiana, Oklahoma, South Carolina, and Virginia.*

Which states restrict the sale of vaults to funeral homes? *Tennessee, possibly others.*

Which state prohibits cemeteries from selling vaults or memorial markers? *New Jersey.*

Which states stipulate that funeral merchandise can only be sold by funeral directors and by no one else? *New York and New Jersey.*

Which states do not allow funeral homes and cemeteries to be owned by the same people? *Michigan, New York, and Wisconsin.*

Which state requires cemeteries to be not-for-profit organizations, partnerships, or proprietorships? *Ohio.*

Which state does not allow the sale of pre-need insurance for a later funeral? *South Carolina.*

In nine states, statutes still require embalming of people who die of certain diseases.

Seven states permit interest to be charged by the funeral home on pre-need funeral or cemetery purchases: *Florida, Illinois, Indiana, Michigan, Nebraska, North Carolina, and Texas. Virginia* specifically forbids such charges.

Many states permit the funeral home to dip into the pre-need trust fund for various purposes. *Colorado,* for example, only requires that 75% be protected, permitting the sales agent or funeral director to pocket a 25% commission.

As of 1997, only seven states had some sort of guarantee fund to protect consumers against default on pre-need trust agreements with a funeral home, in case it is sold to another firm. Here are the seven: *Florida, Indiana, Iowa, Missouri, Oregon, Vermont, and West Virginia.*

Some states require that a funeral director be present at a funeral or a viewing.

In most states, the signature of next of kin must be obtained before an autopsy may be performed, before the deceased may be cremated, before the body may be turned over to a medical school for research purposes; or such provision must have been made in the deceased person's will for any of this to be done with his remains.

Which states permit private burial? Which states permit you to care for your dead, without the help of a funeral director for body disposition, if done within 24 hours? (The following paragraph was accurate as of 1997, but it might not contain current data.)

With the possible exception of eight states, in every other state in the United States, including the District of Columbia, you can care for your own dead, and bury them yourself. (Some statutes limit it to 24 hours after death, others do not mention a time factor.) *Here are the exceptions:*

Connecticut—The statutes conflict with one another in such a way as to limit the rights of individuals to care for the disposition of their dead. *(For more on this, see Lisa Carlson, Caring for Your Dead, pp. 235-236.)*

Delaware—Church groups and individuals might have difficulty caring for their dead. The statute implies that a paid "funeral director" must be involved, yet there are no statutes actually forbidding families or church groups from caring for their dead. This problem may have to be settled in court *(cf. Carlson, pp. 244-245).*

Indiana—A statutory conflict exists in this state. While most statutes recognize the rights of families to control the disposition of a body, one statute does not *(cf. Carlson, pp. 303-304).*

Louisiana—Because the laws are contradictory and invite a court challenge, individuals may not be able to care for their own dead *(cf. Carlson, pp. 332-333).*

Nebraska—Laws are especially problematic

here. Families will find it difficult to care for their dead in this state. In addition, they may be charged for a funeral bill for an estranged relative! Lastly, the funeral must agree with written instructions of the deceased prior to death (*cf. Carlson, pp. 406-407*).

New Hampshire—Older statutes cast doubt on the likelihood of caring for your own dead. A 1996 law clearly recognizes your right to do so; but the earlier conflicting laws are still on the books, thus inviting a court challenge. Committee hearings in 1996 blocked efforts to eliminate the confusion (*cf. Carlson, pp. 421-422*).

New York—These statutes are also limiting. Papers must be obtained from, and signed by, the funeral director,—and that signature will cost the family a nondeclinable fee of $1,025, if New York fees match the national average (*cf. Carlson, pp. 442-443*).

West Virginia—It appears that, in this state, only people who are members of a religious group may care for their own dead (*cf. Carlson, pp. 582-583*).

LEARNING ABOUT THE CONSOLIDATORS

Service Corporation International (SCI), incorporated in 1984, is the largest funeral consolidator (conglomerate) in the world. It is huge. SCI buys up local funeral homes, small and large. Soon afterward, the prices tend to rise. It frequently has the highest prices.

The Loewen Group is the second largest corporate consolidator in North America. Its prices are generally close to those of SCI. Stewart Enterprises is the third large conglomerate.

As the owners of family-owned funeral homes retire, a consolidator buys them out and then raises the prices.

Funeral home charges are today eight to ten times what they were in the 1960s. The increase in profits has been fabulous. SCI, for example, reported a profit margin of 34% for its cemetery (and mausoleum) operations in 1995. Few other firms in America do nearly as well. The same year, SCI reported a profit margin of 22% on its funeral establishments. In 1994, it reported a $1 billion profit for the year! That same year, it took over 15% of the British funeral establishment. By that time, it had already attained 9% of U.S. and 25% of Australian funeral establishments.

By 1995, it had purchased the largest funeral chain in France, with 950 funeral homes, as well as others in Switzerland, Italy, Belgium, the Czech Republic, and Singapore. That year, its total profit increased by a third—to $1.5 billion.

By the next year (1996), its prearranged funeral revenue surpassed $2.3 billion and its prepaid cemetery sales totaled another $251 million.

SCI prefers to buy up six to twelve or more funeral homes, cemeteries, and crematoriums in an area. Then it "clusters" its funeral operations (embalmers, dispatchers, drivers, hearses, limousines, utility cars, office workers) in one central location.

This markedly reduces costs below that of the small, independent operators;—yet SCI charges more than the independents. In Houston, its fees are 75% higher than the average; in Washington, D.C., they are 40% higher.

Prices of Loewen Group mortuaries generally parallel those of SCI. In a late 1990s filing with the Securities and Exchange Commission (SEC), it reported a fabulous gross profit of 41% from its funeral operations (while, the same year, SCI reported an excellent 25.3%).

By the latter part of the 1990s, the consolidators owned only 10% of the funeral homes in the U.S., but those were prime properties which do 20% of the nation's funerals. According to a survey by Memorial Society of North Texas, mortuaries (cemeteries and mausoleums) owned by SCI, Loewen, and Stewart Enterprises, the three largest consolidators, were consistently more expensive than the independents in the area.

In a report to the Securities and Exchange Commission, Loewen commented that the "lack of price sensitivity" by the survivors was one of the "attractive industry fundamentals" of the funeral trade.

Another little trade secret, which greatly helps the conglomerates do so well, is the fact that they are very secretive about the funeral establishments that they own. In an annual financial report to stockholders, SCI included this note: "As an owner of shares in SCI, you are probably aware that the company's name does not appear on any of our family homes or cemeteries." It then goes on to say that stockholders can dial a special phone number and obtain a listing of all the SCI firms, at any one of which they will receive special service. For your information, that number is 1-800-9CARING. It should be able to provide you with names and addresses of SCI mortuaries, as well as price lists, in the area you specify.

You can also obtain a listing of chain-owned mortuaries from funerals.org. But please understand that the rapid rate of acquisitions makes it difficult to keep up with the latest data.

In 1998 the television broadcast, *60 Minutes*, ran a documented story on how prices were raised at a funeral home owned by SCI. Immediately, elsewhere in the nation people began asking funeral homes if they were home-owned. A few began to deny corporate affiliation. One in Oregon was the subject of a lawsuit because of such a denial. It has been reported that Loewen employees are telling those who inquire that the funeral home is "employee-owned," because each worker has a few shares of stock in the firm.

Since the self-contained mortuaries (such as Forest Lawn) have the highest profit margin, there are large bidding wars by the conglomerates to acquire ownership of them.

Here is how some people make a lot of money: They incorporate as a for-profit corporation and, then, build funeral homes on untaxed, church-owned cemetery grounds. By doing this, they are taking an unfair advantage over local funeral home owners who have to pay property taxes for the land on which their buildings rest.

A mortician in Pennsylvania, for example, has

built a mausoleum on the grounds of a church cemetery. He pays no property taxes while collecting all the money from the sale of crypts. When all the spaces are sold, he transfers ownership to the church. Eventually, the church will no longer be able to keep up the place with the small amount of money he has given them for "perpetual care."

THE FEDERAL TRADE COMMISSION'S FUNERAL RULE

Limitations of the funeral rule. In 1975 after a two-year study, the Federal Trade Commission (FTC) issued a "trade rule" that required several things: (1) The consumer would have a right to choose or refuse services such as embalming or grief counseling, with an appropriate reduction in cost for those customers who refused such services. (2) Prices must be quoted over the telephone. (3) Undertakers had to inform customers that embalming was not required by law. (4) The cheapest casket must be displayed with the others. (5) Funeral providers would be prohibited from telling the customer that the 'eternal sealer' casket will preserve the embalmed body for a long or indefinite time.

Such regulations are obviously good ones. But the funeral industry immediately declared outright war against this trade rule. One industry member described it as "a Soviet-style piece staged by the FTC."

The lobbyists did their work well. Within three years, two components of the rule had been omitted: (1) The section requiring undertakers to display their cheapest caskets with the others. (2) The section prohibiting the undertaker from trying to influence the customer's choice of goods and services. Those, of course, were key points.

When public hearings about the final adoption of the rule finally occurred in 1984, consumer advocates stated that only a minimal protection for the bereaved had been left in place.

In the intervening 15 years, even that minimal protection was being ignored. In 1990, the FTC stated that it "makes no effort to ascertain whether funeral establishments are complying with the rule," and that "the rule has not contributed to a general reduction in the price of funerals."

Lisa Carlson, in her book, *Caring for the Dead: Your Final Act of Love*, mentions a survey she conducted of Vermont's 70 funeral homes. She found that none were in full compliance with the FTC's rule.

But, never fear, the funeral homes always win out in the end. In 1996, the FTC and the National Funeral Directors Association (NFDA) struck a new deal. Under the new plan, no longer will funeral homes be subjected to a fine for violating the rule.

Funeral Monitor, an industry trade journal, provided additional details and bragged about the NFDA accomplishment:

"The FTC will no longer publicize the names of funeral homes accused of violating the rule. Funeral homes that violate the rule will be able to avoid a complaint filed in federal court, as well as an injunction against the funeral home and owner."

And, to add insult to injury to the hapless consumers, violators will receive an emblem telling consumers that the establishment is a program participant and has voluntarily agreed to comply with the provisions of the rule.

So they can say they do, when they don't.

The wording of some of these regulatory paragraphs is fabulous. Men must stay up at night thinking them up. Here is the FTC-required statement that every funeral home / mortuary must post in a public place:

"The goods and services shown below are those we can provide to our customers. You may choose only the items you desire. However, any funeral arrangements you select will include a charge for our basic services and overhead."

The above paragraph appears to protect the public, but look at it more closely. This statement was obviously written, not by the FTC, but by the funeral industry!

It is the last sentence that dooms you to the highest add-on charges. *Whether or not you "choose" or "desire" any of the listed "basic services," you will have to pay for all of them.*

Below the above statement is listed a variety of items you will be paying for.

Helpful requirements of the rule. Having said all that, it should be emphasized that the most helpful part of the FTC funeral rule is the regulation requiring funeral directors to provide consumers with specific and detailed price information in advance, so the consumers can then purchase only the funeral merchandise and funeral services they desire.

When a consumer phones a funeral provider and inquires about terms, conditions, or prices of funeral goods or services, the funeral provider is required to give him the prices and any other information from price lists to help answer the questions. He must also give him any other information about prices or offerings that is readily available, and he must reasonably answer his questions. The objective is to enable consumers to comparison-shop by telephone before selecting the funeral home, goods, and services.

Specific prohibitions. The FTC's funeral rule specifically prohibits funeral directors from misrepresenting eight things:

1 - They cannot say that embalming is legally required (except when special circumstances require it). They can never say that embalming is required before cremation.

2 - When there is no open-casket ceremony or viewing, they cannot say that state law requires purchase of a casket for a direct cremation.

3 - They cannot say that the customer is required, by law, to purchase an outer burial container, when that is not the case. Nor can they tell him that a particular cemetery requires a vault when it is not true.

4 - It is illegal to tell the consumer that anything is required by law, when it is not.

5 - They cannot make preservative and protective claims which are not true.

6 - The FTC prohibits all misrepresentations or deceptive practices not specifically prohibited by the funeral rule.

7 - They cannot force the consumer to purchase goods and services which are unwanted and / or not needed as a prerequisite for purchasing other goods and services they may desire. For example, they cannot charge an additional fee or surcharge to a customer who might purchase a casket somewhere else.

8 - They cannot alter prices based on the specific selections a consumer might make.

Inadequate surveilance. Unfortunately, although there are 22,000 funeral homes in the United States, as of 1995 there were only two FTC investigators to investigate reports of violations of the rule. As mentioned earlier, the 1996 Funeral Rule Offenders Program (FROP) permits a funeral home which violates the rule to avoid being punished with anything more than a three-year "probation," and the FTC agrees to keep the names of the offending funeral homes a secret.

THE NEW YORK
CONSUMER AFFAIRS REPORT

Introduction to the Report. On February 11, 1999, Jules Polonetsky, Commissioner of the Department of Consumer Affairs (DCA), released a lengthy report, *The High Cost of Dying*. Here is a brief summary of that report:

The report reveals how changes in the funeral industry are driving up the cost of burying a loved one and proposals to remedy the situation.

According to the report, consumers are paying increasingly exorbitant prices for funerals, due to

deceptive trade practices and the growing monopo-
lization within the funeral industry.

A few funeral conglomerates are buying up the
smaller funeral homes and jacking up prices.

"Prices for funeral services are extortionately
high, and they'll continue to climb for New York
City consumers as long as competition and the
ability to shop around are so seriously impeded
. . Our report also documents how funeral homes
deceive consumers by imposing illegal charges and
pressuring them to purchase services they don't
need.

"The average cost of a funeral in New York City
is $6,700, making it the third largest purchase
most consumers will make during their lifetime.
But unlike shopping for a house or a car, consumers shopping for funerals are in a state of great
emotional vulnerability. As a result, consumers
need an extra level of protection to ensure they're
not targeted for rip-offs."

The conglomerate problem. The report goes
on to discuss Houston-based Service Corporation
International (SCI), which buys up neighborhood
funeral homes (while keeping their original names)
and blocking competition within particular commu-
nities. He noted that SCI-owned funeral homes,
which conduct 13% of all funerals in New York City,
charge 25% more than their independent counterparts.

"SCI is gobbling up funeral homes all over the
city and consumers are paying the price. Instead
of passing on the economies of scale to their customers, SCI is seeing its growing dominance as an
opportunity to both reduce costs and raise prices."

The DCA report also alleges that funeral homes are deliberately hiding the fact that they are owned by large companies. Consumers think they are comparing prices with different companies, when they are all part of the conglomerate.

These firms then make suggestions to the survivors which greatly inflate funeral costs.

"What consumers don't know—and what SCI isn't telling them—is that their neighborhood funeral home which has been around for generations could have been bought by SCI. As a result, the counsel they depend upon from their funeral director could simply be profit-seeking policy directives dictated from Houston."

By state law, caskets can be purchased from outside sources for use at a funeral home. But DCA investigators found that some funeral homes said they would have to charge a $250 "service charge," an illegal fee, if they accept an outside casket. Other illegal methods were also used to circumvent the law about the use of caskets purchased elsewhere.

In order to make more money, a number of funeral homes were using "embalming centers" as a money-saving strategy. Large chains were also doing this. Funeral homes do not disclose that they are shipping the bodies of loved ones here and there to have this done.

Monument (gravestone) dealers have disappeared in the New York City area, so consumers are forced to buy them from the funeral home directors. (Big firms buy them up and then close them down.) In other instances, consumers are charged for monuments which they never ordered.

Five proposals. In his official report, Commissioner Polonetsky offered five proposals to improve New York City regulations that have governed the funeral industry since 1981:

1 - General price list. Funeral homes would be required to post their price lists in a publicly accessible area in the funeral home, so consumers could obtain this general price information without having to sit through a funeral director's sales pitch.

2 - Ownership disclosure. Funeral homes would be required to disclose, on a sign located either immediately outside or inside the front entrance, information about who owns and operates the home.

3 - New monument contracts. Full explanation and prices would be given to the consumer, and he would sign a statement that he was given it. He would also be told that monuments do not have to be purchased at the time the other arrangements are made.

4 - Travel notification. Bodies could not be moved from the funeral home for any reason, without the consumer having first given signed consent.

5 - Annual price survey. DCA would conduct an annual survey of funeral prices and publish them in a brochure.

Whether or not this report resulted in a corrective legislation in New York City, I do not know. But it is unlikely that such recommended regulations are protecting you in your state.

ORGANIZATIONS
THAT CAN HELP YOU

Here is an invaluable collection of names and addresses; some of which you may wish to contact:

• You may want to contact one or more of the memorial societies in your area. (They are listed at the back of this book.) If you have difficulty contacting a local memorial society, contact *Funeral Consumers Alliance* headquarters. You can also enroll as a member of FCA. Here is their phone number: **800-765-0107**. Their address is FCA, P.O. Box 10, Hinesburg, VT 05461. (This organization was formerly called Funeral and Memorial Societies Association; FAMSA). FCA is an excellent source of information on keeping funeral costs reasonable and locating a memorial society near you, which can help provide you with a low-cost funeral.

• The FCA website, posts a listing of chain-owned mortuaries, although the rapid rate of acquisitions makes it difficult to keep track of recent developments. Here is the website:

funerals.org

• You may wish to contact Choice in Dying, Inc. for a current copy of your state's living will and durable power of attorney: Choice in Dying: 475 Riverside Drive, Room 1852, New York, NY 10115. Phones: **800-989-9455** / 212-870-2003. They mail out thousands of copies each year. The cost is $5.00 ppd. for a copy of your state's living will and durable power of attorney. An alternative is to go to their website: **partnershipforcaring.org** and download, free of charge, a copy of your state's living will and durable power of attorney.

You may decide to inquire about their *Living Will Registry*. By joining it, they will ensure that your form is correctly filled out, assign you a registry number, maintain a copy of your living will, and issue you a plastic card which you can carry with you at all times so medical personnel can know where to obtain a copy of your living will and power of attorney authorization. Any current changes you may wish to make can be sent to them. The cost is about $40.

If you are unable to obtain a state-specific-copy of the *Living Will or Durable Power of Attorney for Healthcare*, Choice in Dying can provide it for you. These are critical documents for end-of-life treatment issues that may improve the quality of declining years by allowing a person to express his choices in legally binding documents. A "living will" is a document in which you may designate the treatments you wish to avoid when death is impending. You should know that, even though the deceased made out a living will, it may be ignored by the medical staff at the hospital without an aggressive family member to intervene.

• Henry Wasielewski, of Phoenix, Arizona (a Catholic priest), carries on a personal campaign against the high priced funeral industry. Since he began about 1985, he has obtained the help of a number of friends. He is able to provide you with comparative funeral home and cemetery price lists in various localities. His web address is:

xroads.com/~funerals

• If you want to know which funeral homes and cemeteries are owned by SCI, you can phone one of their offices which will give you that information: **800-9CARING**. As noted earlier, their operations are generally higher priced than others.

• Funeral Help Program (FHP). This is a division of Alzheimer's Research Foundation, Inc. of Virginia, 1236 Ginger Crescent, Virginia Beach, VA 23456. Phone: 877-427-0220. Another phone number is **800-418-0471**. They say they can provide you with caskets, urns, and vaults at average savings of 30% to 60%. Give the model number over the phone, and get cost comparison from a nationwide bank of providers who can provide any model delivered within hours.

• Conference of Funeral Service Examining Boards, 15 Northeast 3rd St., P.O. Box 497, Washington, Indiana 47501. Phone: 812-254-7887. This organization represents the licensing boards of 47 states and it is in charge of dealing with complaints about funeral industry businesses.

• Social Security death benefits. A standard $255.00 burial benefit is available, in addition to a range of benefits for survivors. Contact your local Social Security Office for the proper forms and requirements. You will need a copy of the *Statement of Death by Funeral Director* (sometimes called a *Death Report*). The funeral director will often file this for you.

• "Product Report: *Prepaying Your Funeral?*" *(D13188)*. AARP Fulfillment (EE0139), 601 E Street

NW, Washington, D.C. 20049. Send a postcard and allow six weeks for delivery of this very detailed and informative report.

• For a complete copy of the FTC Funeral Rule, write to: Federal Trade Commission, Room 130, Washington, D.C. 20580, ATTN: Public Reference Branch. Ask for a copy of the FTC Funeral Rule.

• International Order of the Golden Rule, P.O. Box 3586, Springfield, IL 62708. Phone: 217-793-3322. This is an association of about 1500 independent funeral homes. The emphasis is on 'independent' and membership is by invitation only. They can provide you with a list of funeral homes which are not owned by the conglomerates. They consider their member homes to be among the best and most honest in the nation.

• Cremation Association of North America, 401 N. Michigan Ave., Chicago, IL 60611. Phone: 312-644-6610. Send a self-addressed envelope with 85-cents postage, to receive six informative pamphlets on cremation.

• Jewish Funeral Directors of America, Inc., 250 West 57th Street, Suite 2329, New York, NY 10107. Phone: 212-582-9744. JFDA, with approximately 200 members, is the national trade association of Jewish funeral homes. Since the traditional Jewish burial is extremely practical and cost-effective, this could be an excellent source of information on reasonable caskets, etc.

• National Funeral Directors and Morticians Association, 1800 East Linwood Blvd., Kansas City, MO 64109. Phone: 816-921-1800. NFDMA is the national association of Black funeral directors and has about 2000 members.

• Addresses and phone numbers to contact for Veterans Administration benefits are listed in the chapter on *Government Benefits for Deceased U.S. Veterans.*

• Addresses and phone numbers for donating a body or organs will be found in the chapter, *Facts about Organ Donations and Medical Gifts.*

• American Hospice Foundation: 1130 Connecticut Avenue NW, Suite 700, Washington D.C. 20036-4101. Phone: 202-223-0204

• Hospice Association of America: 519 C Street NE, Stanton Park, Washington D.C. 20002-5809. Phone: 202-546-4750.

• National Hospice Organization: 1901 North Moore Street, Suite 901, Arlington, VA 22209. Phone: 703-243-5900.

• Hospice Education Institute, Five Essex Square: P.O. Box 713, Essex, CT 06426 Phone: 800-331-1620.

BOOKS AND OTHER WRITTEN MATERIALS

The book you now have in hand will probably provide you with most of the information you need about funerals, cemeteries, and burials, But there are also a number of other worthwhile books.

• Lisa Carlson's book is excellent. The first edition was printed with the title, *Caring for Your Own Dead*. The new edition, which is now available, is titled, *Caring for the Dead: Your Final Act of Love*. The book lists, state by state, the laws in all the

states where it is legal to by-pass the funeral industry entirely—and directly bury your own dead.
Carlson campaigned strongly against the funeral
industry, and eventually became executive director
of *Funeral and Memorial Societies of America* (now
known as *Funeral Consumers Alliance;* FCA), the
coordinating organization for all the memorial societies. If you wish to purchase a copy of Carlson's
book, phone 800-765-0107 (the FCA office) and
order a copy. The book has 640 pages and costs
$29.95, plus shipping (which in the U.S. is $2.50,
or priority mail $3.95). They accept Visa and
Mastercharge. If you wish to order by mail, their
address is FCA, P.O. Box 10, Hinesburg, VT 05461.

• *Choice in Dying,* a book published by Choice
in Dying, Inc., contains extensive information on living wills and power of attorney. But the sample, state-
specific living wills and power of attorney forms in it
may not be as current as can be obtained by contacting Choice in Dying directly: 475 Riverside Drive,
Room 1852, New York, NY 10115. Phones: **800-989-
9455** / 212-870-2003. Or go to their website:
partnershipforcaring.org.

• The FAMSA Newsletter is a quarterly, published
by the Funeral and Memorial Societies of America
(FAMSA; now called Funeral Consumers Alliance:
FCA). $10 in the U.S., $15 in Canada. P.O. Box 10,
Hinesburg, VT 05461. The latest information on
what is happening to funeral consumers throughout the United States. FAMSA also has a wide selec-
tion of materials on funeral planning.

Here are several fairly current books:

• Kenneth V. Iserson, M.D., *Death to Dust: What Happens to Dead Bodies*, 1994. A remarkably thorough book on what happens to a person in the United States after he dies.

• Andrea Sankar, *Dying at Home: A Family Guide for Caregiving*. How to care for a dying loved one at home.

• Consumers' Reports, *Funerals: Consumers' Last Rites*, 1977. An excellent book on the entire funeral problem in America, and what you can do about it.

• AARP Books, *It's Your Choice*. A good book to assist in preplanning for a funeral.

• Earnest Morgan, *Dealing Creatively with Death: A Manual of Death Education and Simple Burial*, 1998. This is a classic in the field, and discusses living with people who are dying, bereavement, the right to die, simple burial and cremation, death ceremonies, etc.

• T. Patrick Hill and David Shirley, *A Good Death*. This book is published by Choice in Dying, the largest right-to-die organization in the world, and is opposed to keeping tubes in people interminably.

• Pastor William L. Coleman, *It's Your Funeral*. This is an overview of funerals as they relate to religious beliefs down through the centuries.

• Daniel R. Tobin, M.D., *Peaceful Dying*. A guide to preserving your dignity and choice at the end of life.

• Edward A. Martin, *Psychology of Funeral Services*. In this book he describes the marvelous and gullible ignorance of the public, who are able to be fooled by the funeral industry into buying what they do not need. There is a fair amount of information in this book.

• R.E. Markin, *The Affordable Funeral*. A planning book for funeral arrangements.

• Bernice C. Harper, Death: *The Coping Mechanism of the Health Professional*. Discusses the end of life from the standpoint of the attending nurse.

• Darryl J. Roberts, *Profits of Death*. A former funeral director explains how the funeral industry functions.

• Lee Norrgard, *Making End-of-Life Decisions, 1992*. A book you will value. He explains a lot of the fraudulent dealings of the funeral industry. Norrgard was consumer affairs analyst for the American Association of Retired Persons (AARP),

• Marilyn Webb, *The Good Death: The New American Search to Reshape the End of Life*. Another book about the effort to make the last days of the dying better.

• Sandol Stoddard, *The Hospice Movement*. An excellent book on the history and objectives of the hospices, which try hard to provide peaceful final days to the dying.

• June Bingham, et al., *You and the ICU*. The problems you will encounter in the intensive care unit of the hospital, which considers it their duty to keep you stuffed with tubes.

• John H. Eckels, *Mortuary Science*. He describes, in detail, the procedures used behind closed doors in the funeral home and cemetery.

• R. Moroni Leash, MSW [Master of Social Work], *Death Notification: A Practical Guide*, 1994. This was written for professional people, to help them know how to notify next of kin about a person who has just died.

• Michael W. Kubasak, *Cremation and the Funeral Director: Successfully Meeting the Challenge*. This book discusses the value of cremation for the funeral director.

• Thomas Lynch, *The Undertaking: Life Studies from the Dismal Trade*. This book became a best seller in America. It tells about his life as an undertaker in a small Michigan town.

• Jessica Mitford's 1963 book, *The American Way of Death*, and her more recent book, *The American Way of Death Revisited*, discuss problems in the funeral industry.

• Rabbi Arnold M. Goodman, *A Plain Pine Box: A Return to Simple Jewish Funerals and Eternal Traditions*, 1981. The story of one Jewish congregation who decided to offer free funerals to its members and how the local Jewish funeral home divided the Jewish community. Full of helpful details on a group which actually offered free funerals.

Here are additional sources:

• On February 11, 1999, Jules Polonetsky, Commissioner of the Department of Consumer Affairs (DCA), released a lengthy report, *The High Cost of Dying,* in which he showed how changes in the funeral industry are driving up funeral and burial costs.

• A *"60 Minutes"* documentary, dated December 20, 1980, on the subject of the Neptune Society was revealing. You might be able to obtain it.

• *Modern Maturity,* the magazine of the American Association of Retired Persons (AARP), ran a single article in 1996 on problems within the funeral industry.

• *Kiplinger's Personal Finance* and *Kiplinger's Money Magazine* carried stories on the problem in 1997.

• Larry Burkett, founder of Christian Financial Concepts, has commended the work of FCA and its associate societies, and recommends not being in funeral debt.

• From time to time, *Consumers Digest* has an article on the subject.

• Roul Tunley's *"Can You Afford to Die?"* in the June 17, 1961, issue of the *Saturday Evening Post.* This was one of the few press reports on the value of the work being done by the memorial associations.

• Bill Davidson's article, *"The High Cost of Dying,"* appeared in *Collier's* magazine in May 1951.

LIST OF MEMORIAL SOCIETIES

As mentioned at the beginning of this book, there are probably many worthwhile funeral homes. The problem is locating them. The Funeral and Memorial Societies are dedicated to helping you obtain inexpensive funerals or cremations, according to your choice. They conduct regular area price surveys. Some may have negotiated a discount for members. Request a brochure for affordable funeral options. Since most societies are staffed by volunteers, not all the phone numbers in this list may be current.

If you are unable to locate a society in your area, phone the *Funeral Consumers Alliance* (FCA) office at 800-765-0107. It is the central clearing house for the various societies. If there is no society in your general locality, you might wish to consider joining Friends of FCA. They will be able to provide you with certain help until a new society is organized.

— UNITED STATES OF AMERICA —

Alabama

Call the FCA office (800-765-0107)

Alaska

Anchorage—Cook Inlet Memorial   907-566-3732 / P.O. Box 102414, 99510

Arizona

Phoenix—Funeral Consumers Alliance: Central Arizona   480-929-9659 / P.O. Box 0423, Chandler, 85244-0423

Prescott—Memorial Society of Prescott 520-778-3000 / P.O. Box 1090, 86302-1090

Tucson—Funeral Consumers Alliance of Southern Arizona 520-721-0230 / P.O. Box 12661, 85732-2661

Arkansas

Fayetteville—Funeral Consumers Alliance, NW Arkansas 501-582-1631 / P.O. Box 3055, 72702-3055

Little Rock—Memorial Society of Arkansas 501-562-6361 or 888-278-7556 / 11621 Hilaro Springs Road, 72206

California

Arcata/Eureka—Humboldt Funeral Society 707-822-8599 / P.O. Box 856, Arcata 95518

Bakersfield—Kern Memorial Society 661-854-5689 or 661-366-7266 / P.O. Box 1202, 93302-1202

Berkeley—Bay Area Funeral Society 510-841-6653 / P.O. Box 264, 94701-0264

Cotati—Redwood Funeral Society 707-568-7684 / P.O. Box 7501, 94931-7501

Fresno—Valley Memorial Society 559-268-2181 / P.O. Box 101, 93707-0101

Los Angeles—Los Angeles Funeral Society 626-683-3545 or 626-683-3752 / P.O. Box 92313, Pasadena, CA 91109

Modesto—Stanislaus Memorial Society 209-521-7690 / P.O. Box 4252, 95352-4252

Palo Alto—Funeral Consumers Alliance of San Mateo and Santa Clara 650-321-2109 or 888-775-5553 / P.O. Box 60448, 94306-0448

Sacramento—Funeral Consumers Alliance, North CA 916-451-4641 / P.O. Box 161688, 95816-1688

San Diego—San Diego Memorial Society 858-874-7921 / 4883 Ronson Ct., Ste. L, 92111-1812

San Luis Obispo—Central Coast Memorial Society 805-543-6133 / P.O. Box 679, 93406-0679

Santa Barbara—Funeral Consumers Alliance, Channel Cities 805-640-0109 or 800-520-PLAN / P.O. Box 1778, Ojai, CA 93024-1778

Santa Cruz—Funeral Consumers Alliance of Monterey Bay 831-426-3308 or 866-426-3308 / P.O. Box 2900, 95063-2900

Stockton—Funeral Consumers Alliance, San Joaquin 209-465-2741 / P.O. Box 4832, 95204-4832

Colorado

Denver—Funeral Consumers Society of Colorado 303-759-2800 or 888-438-6431 / 4101 E. Hampden Ave., 80222

Connecticut

Bridgewater—Funeral Information Society of Connecticut 860-355-4197 or 800-607-2801

/ P.O. Box 34, 06752

Delaware

Served by Memorial Society of Maryland

District of Columbia

Washington, D.C.—Memorial Society of Metro-
politan Washington   202-234-7777 / 1500
Harvard St. NW, 20009

Florida

Cocoa—Funeral Consumers Association, Brevard
County   321-242-1421 or 321-255-2100 / P.O.
Box 276, 32923-0276

DeBary—Funeral Society of Mid-Florida   904-
789-1682 or 407-668-6822 / P.O. Box 392,
32713-0392

Deerfield Beach—Funeral Consumers of S.E.
Florida   954-429-0280 or 888-288-9676 / Ste.
144, 1626 SE 3rd Ct., 33441

Ft. Myers—Funeral and Memorial Society of
Southwest Florida   941-573-0507 / P.O. Box
7756, 33911-7756

Gainesville—Memorial Society of Alachua County
352-337-0460 / P.O. Box 14662, 32604-4662

Orlando—Funeral Consumers Alliance, Orlando
407-677-5009 / P.O. Box 953, Goldenrod, FL
32733-0953

Pensacola and Fort Walton Beach—Funeral and
Memorial Society, Pensacola and West Florida
850-477-9085 / 5425 Dynasty Dr., 32504

Sarasota—Funeral Consumers Alliance,

Sarasota-Manatee 941-953-3740 / P.O. Box 15833, 34277-5833

St. Petersburg—Suncoast-Tampa Bay Memorial Society 727-520-8922 / 719 Arlington Ave. North, 33701

Tallahassee—Funeral Consumers Association, Leon County 850-224-2082 / 1006 Buena Vista Dr., 32304

Tampa—Funeral Consumers Association, Tampa Bay 813-948-1990 / 18902 Arbor Dr., Lutz, 33549-5051

Georgia

Atlanta—Memorial Society of Georgia 404-634-2896 or 800-840-4339 / 1911 Cliff Valley Way NE, 30329

Macon—Middle Georgia Chapter use the 800# / 5276 Zebulon Road, 31210

Hawaii

Honolulu—Memorial Society of Hawaii 808-589-2884 / 505 Ward Ave., Suite 203, 96814

Idaho

Boise—Funeral Consumers Alliance of Idaho 208-426-0032 / P.O. Box 1919, 83701-1919

Illinois

Chicago—Chicago Memorial Association 773-238-3746 / P.O. Box 2923, 60690-2923

Urbana—Funeral Consumers of Champaign County / 309 West Green St., 61801

Indiana

Bloomington—Funeral Consumers Alliance,

Bloomington   812-335-6633 / 2661 Fairoaks Dr., 47401

Indianapolis—Indianapolis Memorial Society 317-844-1371 / 5805 East 56th St., 46226

Valparaiso—Memorial Society of Northwest Indiana 219-464-3024 / P.O. Box 329, 46384-0329

Iowa

Iowa City—Memorial Society of Iowa River Valley 319-338-2637 / 120 North Dubuque St., 52245

For all other areas, call the FCA office (800-765-0107)

Kansas

Check Missouri or call the FCA office (800-765-0107)

Kentucky

Louisville—Memorial Society of Greater Louisville 502-454-4855 / P.O. Box 5326, 40255-5326

Louisiana

Baton Rouge—Memorial Society of Greater Baton Rouge / 8470 Goodwood Ave., 70806

Maine

Auburn—Funeral Consumers Alliance of Maine 207-786-4323 or 800-218-9885 / P.O. Box 3122, 04212-3122

Maryland

Bethesda—Funeral Consumers Alliance, MD 301-564-0006 / 9601 Cedar Lane, 20814

Massachusetts

Boston—The Memorial Society 617-859-7990 888-666-7990 / 66 Marlborough St., 02116

East Orleans—Funeral Consumers Alliance, Cape Cod 508-862-2522 or 800-976-9552 / P.O. Box 1375, 02643-1375

New Bedford—Memorial Society of SE Mass. 508-996-0046 / 71 Eighth St., 02740

Springfield—Memorial Society of Western Mass. 413-783-7987 / P.O. Box 2821, 01101-2821

Michigan

Ann Arbor—Memorial Advisory and Planning Society 734-665-9516 / 2030 Chaucer Dr., 48103

Detroit—Greater Detroit Memorial Society 313-886-0998 / P.O. Box 24054, 48224-4054

Flint—Memorial Society of Flint / P.O. Box 4315, 48504-4315

For all other areas, call the FCA office (800-765-0107)

Minnesota

St. Cloud—Minnesota Funeral and Memorial Society   320-252-7540 / 717 Riverside Dr. SE, 56304

Mississippi

Call the FCA office (800-765-0107)

Missouri

Kansas City—Funeral Consumers Alliance, Greater Kansas City 816-561-6322 / 4501 Walnut St., 64111

Montana

Billings—Memorial Society of Montana 406-252-5065 / 1024 Princeton Ave., 59102

Missoula—Five Valleys Memorial Society 406-728-6248 / 405 University Ave., 59801

Nebraska

Call the FCA office (800-765-0107)

Nevada

Reno—Funeral Consumer Information of Nevada 775-329-7705 / P.O. Box 8413, University Station, 89507-8413

New Hampshire

Epping—Memorial Society of New Hampshire 603-679-5721 / P.O. Box 941, 03042-0941

New Jersey

Cherry Hill—Memorial Society of South Jersey 856-235-2783 / 401 Kings Highway North, 08034

East Brunswick—Raritan Valley Memorial Society 732-572-1470 / 176 Tices Lane, 08816

Lincroft—Memorial Association of Monmouth County 732-747-7950 / 1475 West Front St., 07738

Madison—Morris Memorial Society 973-540-9140 / P.O. Box 509, 07940-0509

Montclair—Funeral Consumers Alliance, Essex 973-783-1145 / P.O. Box 1327, 07042-1327

Paramus—Central Memorial Society 201-385-4153 / 156 Forest, 07652

Plainfield—Memorial Society of Plainfield 908-889-6289 / 724 Park Ave., 07060

Princeton—Princeton Memorial Association 609-430-7250 / 50 Cherry Hill Dr., 08540

New Mexico

Albuquerque—Funeral Consumers Alliance, North NM 505-296-5902 / P.O. Box 53464, 87153

Las Cruces—Memorial and Funeral Society of South NM 505-526-7761 / P.O. Box 6531, 88006-6531

New York

Albany—Memorial Society of Hudson-Mohawk Region 518-465-9664 / 405 Washington Ave., 12206-2604

Binghamton—Southern Tier Memorial Society / c/o Haesler, 300 Fordham Road, Vestal, 13850

Buffalo—Greater Buffalo Memorial Society 716-837-8636 / 695 Elmwood Ave., 14222-1601

Corning—Memorial Society of Greater Corning 607-962-7132 or 607-962-1554 / P.O. Box 23, Painted Post, 14870

Ithaca—Ithaca Memorial Society 607-273-8316 / P.O. Box 134, 14851-0134

Long Island—Funeral Consumers Aliance, L.I./ NYC 631-544-0383 / P.O. Box 701, Greenlawn, 11740-0701

New Hartford—Mohawk Valley Memorial Society 315-797-2396 or 315-735-6268 / P.O. Box

322, 13413-0322

Poughkeepsie—Mid-Hudson Memorial Society
914-229-0241 / 249 Hooker Ave., 12603

Rochester—Rochester Memorial Society 716-
461-1620 / 220 Winton Road South, 14610

Syracuse—Syracuse Memorial Society 315-446-
0557 / P.O. Box 67, De Witt, 13214-0067

Yorktown Heights—Funeral Consumers Information Society / Westchester 914-285-0585 / 460
York Ct., 10598-3726

North Carolina

Asheville—Blue Ridge Memorial Society 828-669-
2587 / P.O. Box 2601, 28802-2601

Chapel Hill—Funeral Consumers Alliance, Tri-
angle 919-834-6898 / 1507 Doughton St.
Raleigh, 27608-2821

Charlotte—Funeral Consumers Alliance Center
704-596-1208 / P.O. Box 26507, 28221

Wilmington—Memorial Society of Coastal Carolina 910-458-4136 / P.O. Box 4262, 28406-
4262

North Dakota

See South Dakota

Ohio

Akron—Memorial Society of Akron-Canton Area
330-836-4418 or 330-849-1030 / 3300
Morewood Road, 44333

Cincinnati—Memorial Society of Greater Cincinnati 513-651-0909 / 536 Linton St., 45219

Cleveland—Cleveland Memorial Society 216-751-5515 / 21600 Shaker Blvd., Shaker Heights, 44122

Columbus—Memorial Society of the Columbus Area 614-263-4632 / P.O. Box 14835, 43214-4835

Toledo—Funeral Consumers Alliance, Northwest Ohio 419-874-6666 / 2210 Collingwood Blvd., 43620-1147

Oklahoma

Ardmore—FCA of SW   800-371-2221 / 1550 Knox Road, 73401

Oregon

Portland—Oregon Memorial Association 503-297-3513 or 888-475-5520 / P.O. Box 25578, 97298

Pennsylvania

Erie—Memorial Society of Erie 814-456-4433 / P.O. Box 3495, 16508-3495

Harrisburg—Memorial Society of Greater Harrisburg 717-564-8507 / 1280 Clover Lane, 17113

Philadelphia—Funeral Consumers Alliance, Philadelphia 215-545-9210 / 1906 Rittenhouse Sq., 19103-5793

Pittsburgh—Pittsburgh Memorial Society 412-621-4740 / 543 Neville St., 15213

State College—Memorial Society of Central Pennsylvania 814-237-7605 / 780 Waupelani Dr., 16801

Rhode Island

East Greenwich—Memorial Society of Rhode
Island 401-884-1227 / 119 Kenyon Ave.,
02818

South Carolina

Columbia—Funeral Consumers Alliance of South
Carolina 803-772-7054 / 2701 Heyward St.,
29205

South Dakota

Lemmon—Funeral Consumer Information Society
of the Dakotas 605-374-5336 / 19168 Flat
Creek Road, 57638

Tennessee

Chattanooga—Memorial Society of Chattanooga
423-886-3480 / 3224 Navajo Dr., 37411

Knoxville—East Tennessee Memorial Society
865-483-4843 / P.O. Box 10507, 37939

Memphis—Funeral Consumers Alliance, Mid
South 901-685-2464 or 901-680-9149 / P.O.
Box 770388, 38177

Nashville—Funeral Consumers Alliance, Middle
Tenn. 615-907-3364 or 888-254-3872 / 1808
Woodmont Blvd., 37215

Texas

Amarillo, El Paso, Lubbock, Rio Grand Valley—
Funeral Consumers Alliance of Southwest
800-371-2221 (TX/OK) / 2875 E. Parker Road,
Plano, 75074

Austin—Austin Memorial and Burial Information
Society 512-480-0555 / P.O. Box 4382,
78765-4382

Commerce, Dallas, Denton, Fort Worth, Longview, Tyler—Funeral Consumers Alliance of North Texas   972-509-5686 or 800-371-2221 / 2875 E. Parker Rd., Plano 75074

Corpus Christi—Memorial Society of Southern Texas   1-800-371-2221 / 3125 Home Road, 78415

Houston—Funeral Consumer Alliance, Houston   713-526-4267 or 888-282-4267/ 5200 Fannin St., 77004-5899

San Antonio—San Antonio Memorial Society 210-341-2213 / 7150 Interstate 10 West, 78213

Waco—Memorial Society of Northern Texas, Central Texas Chapter (TX/OK) 1-800-371-2221 / 4209 North 27th St., 76708-1509

Utah

Orem—Funeral Consumers Alliance of Utah 801-226-4701 / 1823 S 250 E, 84058-7840

Vermont

East Montpelier—Funeral Consumers Alliance, Vermont   802-476-4300 or 800-805-0007 / 1630 Clark Rd., 05651

Virginia

Arlington—Memorial Society of Northern Virginia   703-271-9240 / 4444 Arlington Blvd., 22204

Charlottesville—Memorial Planning Society of Piedmont 804-293-8179 / 717 Rugby Road, 22903

Virginia Beach—Memorial Society of Tidewater   757-428-5134 / P.O. Box 4621, 23454-4621

Washington

Seattle—People's Memorial Association 206-325-0489 / 2366 Eastlake Ave. E., Areis Bldg. #409, 98102

Spokane—Spokane Memorial Association 509-924-8400 / P.O. Box 13613, 99213-3613

Yakima—Funeral Association of Central Washington 509-248-4533 / P.O. Box 379, 98907

West Virginia

Lewisburg—Memorial Society of Greenbrier Valley / P.O. Box 1277, 24901

Morgantown and NE area—Call MD 800-564-0017

Wisconsin

Appleton—Funeral Consumers Alliance—Fox Valley 920-731-5672 / P.O. Box 1422, 54912-1422

Milwaukee—Funeral Consumer Information Society 262-238-0507 or 800-491-8150 / 13001 W. North Ave., Brookfield, 53005

Wyoming

Call the FCA office (800-765-0107)

— CANADA —

Alberta

Calgary—Calgary Co-op Memorial Society 403-248-2044 / 216 Marpole Bay NE, 52A 4W9

Edmonton—Memorial Society of Edmonton and District 403-944-0196 / 10242-105th St., T5J 3L5

Red Deer—Memorial Society of Red Deer and District 403-340-1021 / P.O. Box 817, T4N 5H2

British Columbia

Vancouver—Area Memorial Society of British Columbia 604-527-1012 / #212 - 624 Sixth St., New Westminster, V3L 3C4

Manitoba

Winnipeg—Funeral Planning / Memorial Society of Manitoba 204-452-7999 / 661 Jubilee Ave., 43L 105

New Brunswick

Fredericton—Memorial Society of New Brunswick / P.O. Box E3B 5A6

Ontario

Guelph—Memorial Society of Guelph 519-822-7430 / P.O. Box 1784, N1H 7A1

Hamilton—Funeral Advisory Society of Hamilton District 905-389-8240 / P.O. Box 89026, L8S 4R5

Kingston—Memorial Society of Kingston 613-531-8948 / c/o Burdsall, 960 Killarney Cr., K7M 8C6

Kitchener—Memorial Society of Kitchener-Waterloo 519-579-3800 or (Cambridge) 519-653-5705 / P.O. Box 113, N2G 3W9

London—Memorial Society of London 519-472-0670 / P.O. Box 1729, N6A 5H9

Niagara—Niagara Peninsula Memorial Society 905-358-5060 / P.O. Box 21021, L2E 6Z2

Ottawa—Ottawa Memorial Society 613-828-4926 / 1903-1025 Richmond Road, KZB 8G8

Peterborough—Funeral Planning Association 705-742-0550 / P.O. Box 1795, K9J 7X6

Sudbury—Memorial Society of Northern Ontario 705-673-5532 / c/o Maitland, 384 Van Home St., P3B 1J3

Thunder Bay—Memorial Society of Thunder Bay 801-683-3051 / P.O. Box 501, P7C 424

Toronto—Area Funeral Advisory and Memorial Society 416-241-6274 / Saint Phillips St., Etobicoke, M9P 2N8

Windsor—Memorial Society of Windsor District 519-969-6767 or 519-966-1064 / P.O. Box 481, N9A 6M6

Quebec

Montreal—L'Association Commemorative Funeraire de Montreal 514-485-8527 / P.O. Box 881, NDG Sub H4A 3S3

Saskatchewan

Lloydminster—Lloydminster-Vermilion Memorial Society 306-825-3769 / 4805 47th St., S9V 9K2

Saskatoon—Memorial Society of Saskatchewan 306-374-5190 / P.O. Box 1846, S8L 3S2

INDEX

A

"Abandoned" grave lots 68
Acknowledgment notes 56
Acreage costs 69
Advance (medical) directives
   15, 16, 17, 18, 21, 26
Announcement cards 56
Antibiotics 22
Ashes 74, 75

B

Batesville Casket Company
   64
Billing clause 89
Bodily integrity 21, 22
Body donation 129
Books 159
Burial clothing 56
Burial permit 57
Burial plots 65
By-pass funeral industry 103

C

Cash advance items 89
Casket markup 63
Casket price list 58
Caskets 38, 39
Catheters 12
Cemeteries 34
Cemetery fees 56, 70
Chapel 57

Choice in Dying, Inc.
   19, 23, 156, 160
Church funeral committee 126
Clergy 55
Clergy honorarium 56, 57
Closing the grave 67
Coffin-makers' association 35
Conglomerate 145, 152
Congress 33, 34
Consolidators 77, 145
Constructive delivery 91
Contract cancellation 92
CPR 21
Cremation 72, 83, 134
Cremation and Bible 85, 86
Cremation casket 72
Cremation chamber 73
Cremation containers 74
Cremation process 73
Crematories 73, 84, 115
Cruzan decision 15, 17
Crypts 34, 70

D

Death care stocks 34
Death certificate 57, 118
Death-benefit payments 37
Default guarantees 92
Defibrillating machine 13
Denver cremation fees 80

Denver prices 63
Die at home, request to 22
Direct cremation 84
Direct cremation firms 76
DNR order 21, 22
Do not resuscitate 21, 22
Donated body 84
Draining the trusts 92
Durable health-care power of attorney 19
Durable power of attorney 17, 19, 20, 156
Durable power of attorney authorization 19
Dying at home, requested 23

E

Embalming 49
Embalming procedure 52
Embalming school 52
Estate 24
External pacemaker 13

F

Family burial plot 110
FAMSA 155, 160
FCA 155
Federated Funeral Directors of America 60
Feeding tube 11, 22
Flower stands 57
Flowers 54, 57
Force feeding 12, 27
Formaldehyde 54
Fraud—*see Scams*
Funeral and Memorial Societies Association (FAMSA) 155
Funeral checklist 100
Funeral committee 126
Funeral Consumers Alliance (FCA) 155, 160, 165
Funeral home 33, 34, 36
Funeral home vehicles 56
Funeral industry 34
Funeral prices 58
Funeral rule, FDA 45-46, 50, 147, 151, 158

G

General price list 58
Graveside procedure 67
Graveside services 56
Guest registers 56

H

Hardwood caskets 38
Health-care proxy 16
Hearse 56
Homemade casket 107-108
Hospice 30
Hospices 23, 28, 159
Houston add-ons 63
Houston basic crypt 71
Houston price range 61

I

Immediate need sales 65
Informed consent 14, 21, 22
Insurance benefits 37
Insurance policy, pre-need 94
Intensive care unit 13
Interest charges, pre-need 92

Interfaith Funeral Information
    Committee (IFIC) 60
Intravenous lines 22
Irrevocable contracts,
    pre-need 93
Irrevocable trust 25

J

Jewish burials 87

L

Law 47
Lawn-type cemetery 69
Legal proxy 19, 21
Living trusts 24, 25
Living will 15, 16, 18, 19, 20,
    21, 156
Living will registry 156
Loewen Group 45, 145

M

Mausoleums 34, 69
Mechanical breathing
    machine 22
Medicaid 15, 21
Medicaid limits 88
Medical gifts 129
Medical school 84
Medicare 15, 21
Memorial 66
Memorial gardens 66
Memorial societies 137, 165
Missouri vs. Cruzan 15
Model changes 91
Monuments (gravestone) 56
Morgue 52

N

Nasogastric tube 12
National Burial Case Associa-
    tion 35
National cemetery 37, 135-136
National Funeral Directors
    Association 60
Neptune Society 78, 80
New York Report 151
Next of kin 53, 54, 116
Non-funeral home cremation
    115
Nondeclinable fee 59
Nursing home, selecting 30

O

Obituary notice 55, 57, 116
Opening the grave 67
Oral intubation 11
Organ donations 130, 133
Organ transplants 130
Organizations 155
Outer burial container price
    list 58

P

Pacemakers 13, 115
Pallbearers 57
Patient Self-Determination Act
    15, 20, 23
Pay-ahead plans 87
Perpetual care 68, 70, 71
Planning funeral service 99
Power of attorney—*see
    durable power of
    attorney*

Prayer cards 56
Preparation room 52
Pricing formulas 41
Private burial 110
Private burial plot 110
Private casket 108
Private cemetery 114
Private funeral 103, 117
Private funeral procedure 104
Probate 24
Protective caskets 42

Q

Queen Elizabeth I 44

R

Registry 128
Rented caskets 81
Respirator 11, 13, 27
Revocable trust 25

S

Salesman 35
Scams 26, 96, 97
Sealer caskets 42
Sealer Vaults 49
Self-determination 21, 22
Service Corporation International (SCI) 77, 80, 145, 153, 157
Services, funeral 56
Social Security death benefits 157
Social Security payment 37
State law(s) 17, 18, 19, 20, 21, 47, 74, 140
State-approved living will 23

State-approved power of attorney 23
Stationery 56
Steel caskets 38
Stewart Enterprises 145
Stocks, funeral home 34
Supreme Court 15, 17

T

Thank you cards 56
Total parenteral nutrition 12
Totten trust 95
Trade union benefits 37
Transportation expenses 56
Trocar 54
Tubes 11, 13, 27

U

U.S. Standard Certificate of Death 118
Undertaker 35
Uniform donor card 130
Urn 76
Urn prices 81
Urn vault 76

V

Vaults 46, 60
Ventilator 11
Ventilator tubes 11
Veteran's benefits 37, 135
Viewing 54, 58
Visitation 57
Visitation room 58

W

Washington, D.C. price list 62
Workmen's compensation 37